CHILDREN IN THE HEART

# Children in the Heart of God

**DAVE GIDNEY**

EASTBOURNE

ISBN 1 84291 047 7

Published by
KINGSWAY COMMUNICATIONS LTD
Lottbridge Drove, Eastbourne BN23 6NT, England.
Email: books@kingsway.co.uk

Book design and production for the publishers by
Bookprint Creative Services, P.O. Box 827, BN21 3YJ, England.
Printed in Great Britain.

*To Hannah Reed*
*who taught me the value of a child's faith.*

# *Contents*

# Introduction

At first, church was fun, with lots of games, sweets, and people to play with. Funny old ladies told us stories, and I could get up and run around when all the big people sat down and it got very boring. Sometimes Mummy and Daddy got cross with me and, with red faces, pulled me out of the room. Then they started that funny whispered shouting that grown-ups do, but they would still let me run around outside, or up and down the corridor if it was raining. That could be fun too.

Then school happened. It wasn't so bad after I realised that Mummy or Daddy was going to come back for me every time, but church started to be like school too. There was still the boring bit at the beginning, but now I was older I was supposed to sit still, or stand up. I never knew when they wanted me to do either; I was usually just yanked up and down by my arm. I wished they would make up their minds. Worse still, I was supposed to join in with whatever the really embarrassing person at the front was talking about, and answer his silly questions.

One of the men who sometimes stood up was quite funny.

At one point in the boring bit he would say 'and now children'. Well actually, they all did that, but most of them seemed to want to pat us on the head and show us odd things out of a bag and ramble on for a bit. But this man told us great stories. I wished he had just stopped with the stories though, because then he would ramble on about something else afterwards for ages (well five minutes or so) before letting us all go and sit down again. Then came the moment of relief when we were allowed to go to our classes. There would be sweets and prizes, games and stories. It's funny really, but the boring bit always seemed to go on much longer than this bit.

Then I moved up into secondary school. Church got a bit more boring. I was supposed to look interested in the service and join in even more with the stupid things that the man did in the children's talk. He was so patronising, treating us like little kids. The hymns were old-fashioned, with no beat to them and stupid words. The hymn books were great to fiddle with, except you had to make sure that the little pile of bits (which had somehow been pulled off) got pushed under the seat in front before you sat down again. I used to get a cross look from Dad quite often about that.

I used to be allowed to sit by my friends in church – well sort of friends anyway. I would never hang out with them in the street, or allow my mates to know about them, but they were OK for a Sunday. Now I had been banned from sitting with them, because people said we made too much noise. (Cheek! We were only whispering, and it was very funny.) We still had to go out to Sunday school too. They didn't want us in there with the grown-ups; we were 'too noisy', 'too young' and all sorts of other things. So they sent us out to silly old Sunday school. We didn't even get sweets any more, and as for the teacher . . . well!

By the time I was fourteen, I was too old for Sunday

school, and was told I had to sit in the service. Now I saw what Mum and Dad had been doing all those years. It was boring! Bring back Sunday school. The person at the front would rant and rave about something for about half an hour, waving his Bible around, but I never had a clue what he meant. Then after church, Mum or Dad would ask me what he had said, as though they were testing me. I soon learned to listen to people on the way out of church and repeat those comments to Mum and Dad. It kept them happy.

As for me, well I made up games . . . how many times the man said 'Um' or how many times in a minute he would push his glasses up, or take them off. You know the sort of thing. Of course, I never told my mates; they would have laughed at me or, even worse, done what we did to Geoff the geek at school!

By the time I was sixteen I had had enough. I was doing a Saturday job by now, had finished my GCSEs and decided that was it. Mum and Dad were all very well, but this church business had got to stop. We had a blazing row about it, which went on for weeks, but in the end they gave in, and apart from some subtle attempts at blackmail now and again, they stopped bothering me about it.

Now I am married, with children of my own. I don't inflict church on them like my mum and dad did to me. I think it's mean. The church does not care about them, and God doesn't seem to care either. 'I have tried God and church, and it doesn't work for me, thank you' is what I say when the religious people call at my door.

\* \* \*

Does any of this sound at all familiar? Does this describe attitudes that you know of? Can you recognise your own church or family here?

I hope not. This is meant to be a caricature based on gross generalisations rather than reality, showing the failures of the previous two generations in reaching out to their children. But it does illustrate the problem that churches currently face. Are we going to perpetuate the myth that this hypothetical person has come to believe in? Or are we today going to take our children and their faith more seriously?

Where has the church gone wrong, and how do we fix it? We need to face up to these crucial questions, or many of the smaller churches alive today will be closed within the next 30 years. Doom and gloom? Look at the state of the churches in your own area.

So . . . where does this book fit in? Reaching children for God is a subject that I hope is important to you as a reader. At least if you are not involved yourself you may be seriously considering getting someone to do it in your church. Perhaps you are already an evangelist and have worked with kids before. I hope there are many parents reading this as well, because you are the best evangelists we have. If you are not a parent, then when you have read this, pass it on to someone who is.

This book is meant to be a biblical critique of children's work in Britain today, in the light of specific Old Testament teaching relating to children. I am writing it out of a conviction that we got things quite badly wrong in the twentieth century, and need to have a fairly drastic re-think of what we do. The book suggests that there are many reasons for the mistakes we have made, some of which belong to changes in society, some to wrong theological thinking, and others merely to bad habits. Apportioning blame for these faults is irrelevant; putting them right is what matters. All of these faults can be identified and rectified by bringing them under the authority of the Bible, and especially the Old Testament.

As a father, I confess I have made many mistakes in parenting my own children, and I have fallen into most of the traps and difficulties that I mention in this book. As parents, look to what you can change, not to the embarrassments of the past.

As a child evangelist for the past 20 years, again I have to confess to many mistakes and poor attitudes. This book stems from a reflection on those mistakes, and attempts to correct them in the light of biblical teaching.

As a theologian, I have also written this book for church leaders, looking honestly to try to develop God's teachings in an area that has mainly been ignored, alongside the practical issues of reaching children. It is the Bible that gives us our foundations.

If theology is not something that excites you, if you are not prepared to think deeply about the issues of faith, then perhaps you need to read from Part Two onwards (and hopefully you will feel brave enough to tackle the earlier chapters afterwards). If, as a theologian and possibly church leader, you need to know what biblical base there might be for a work like this one, then the first three chapters are for you.

Whichever of these groups you fit into, read, pray, and ask God to speak to you and help you understand how to live around the children he has called you to serve. Examine what is written here, test it, talk about it with people whose judgement you respect. Then, if God challenges you, ACT!

*Part One*

# THE THEOLOGY OF CHILDREN

# 1

# *The Place of Children in the Heart of God*

The phrase 'God so loved the world' is well known, and is usually taken to include children as well as adults in its sweeping sentiment, but it is a very general statement. Does God have a special regard for children as individuals, or only in so far as they are part of the world and will one day grow up into it? As far as Judaism is concerned, children have always been vitally important, as the Mishnah and Talmud show clearly in several passages. It is also clear from books such as Proverbs, Ecclesiasticus and Wisdom of Solomon[1] that Judaism, in the Old Testament, is modelled on the values of God. Therefore the way it values its children mirrors the value that God places on them.

In this chapter we will first look at what the Bible considers 'the father heart of God'. God stands as the ideal father in his

---

1 See *The Illustrated Bible Dictionary* (IVP, 1980). The word *Talmud* is used in Judaism to refer to the collection of commentaries on the Mishnah. The Mishnah itself is a collection of oral legal teachings about the law of Moses. Ecclesiasticus is one of the apocryphal books of the Jewish period.

relationship to the nation Israel. This holds up an awesome standard for parents to attain to. It does, however, draw a more adequate picture of how God feels, in case our own fathers have not been all that they might have been.

Following that, we will examine the idea that God has a heart for children in particular. Here we will look at the way God has employed children in the Old Testament, and seems to delight to employ them still.

Finally we will consider the idea that children are seen as a blessing from God.

## 1. The role of the ideal father

'The LORD your God carried you, as a father carries his son, all the way you went' (Deuteronomy 1:31). God relates to the nation of Israel as father. He regularly calls Israel his children (for example, Isaiah 45:11). As we trace the history of the nation down through the millennia, Israel becomes an amazing illustration of how caring and patient God is as a father.

It has not been an easy ride for him as a parent. God has had to forgive Israel countless times for just about every problem imaginable (and one or two unimaginable ones), and he even had to throw Israel out of the house (the land) at one point, by way of discipline, before restoring the nation once more. It also suggests something about the way he views children. To use the metaphor of 'child' for Israel, his precious if precocious prodigy, suggests he understands and cares for children in a special way.

### (a) God as a parent

The way God acts as a parent to his children is a helpful model for us as parents. Listed below are some of the qualities of God's character and how they affect his relationship with children in particular.

*(i) Justice*   God is a God of justice (Psalm 89:14). This is a fundamental part of God's character and it affects everything he does. He wants to see justice in operation in the world, and he especially wants to see it demonstrated among his people. He gets particularly aggressive towards those who fail to show justice, and rewards those who do, as for example in Solomon's special role as king, which was to maintain justice (1 Kings 10:9). God is consistent: his values and expectations do not change, and God himself does not change. What is right is rewarded consistently, and what is wrong is punished consistently. In the Old Testament justice becomes something everyone has to follow if they want to stay right with God.

God's justice is also significantly different from all the religious ideas of the other nations around at the time, who had gods that were erratic and unreliable. Chemosh (a Moabite god), for instance, could be helpful and considerate one day and vicious and cruel the next, with no warning and no reason. God, with his insistence on justice, remained reliable. It did not mean that God could not act in violence and judgement, and that disasters could not happen. It was merely that when they did, there was a reason for it which could usually be seen and understood. You knew where you were with Israel's God.

God knows his children, and what they need. As children of God, we expect justice from him, and the children we relate to expect it from us. A common cry from a child towards adults and other children is 'That's not fair!' They have a highly developed sense of fairness, and can often be justified in their cry. When we are standing before God, however, that complaint is never justified, and when we calm down a little, we know it to be the case. If we want to be the sort of parent God is, then justice for our children is something we need to consider very carefully.

*(ii)  Love*   There can be no doubt that God loves us. He has demonstrated that love both to Israel and to the church time and time again in history. Perhaps the greatest passages about this love are found in Hosea chapters 1–3, and chapter 11. Isaiah also sums it up well when he says, 'Can a mother forget the baby at her breast and have no compassion on the child she has borne? Though she may forget, I will not forget you' (Isaiah 49:15).

We are all familiar with this idea that God is a God of love, yet we often fail to comprehend it. We are happy to think in general terms about it, because we suggest then that God will only let 'nice' things happen to us. We often have a soppy sentimental view and forget the true value or cost of love. God is dedicated to us, and to making sure that only the best things happen to us.

This can be a painful love, as it is only those closest to you who might be free to criticise you over a certain problem or habit. Similarly, love can lead us to hurt another person for the same sort of reason. Any parent knows of the love that leads us to deny the child something which is unsuitable, even though it is the only thing that the child wants in the world – for the next hour or two anyway. All parents also know the pain of dragging the child unwillingly to the dentist or doctor, knowing it will be best for them. God's love for his children sometimes had to take this form in the Old Testament. Yet even in the times when he had to punish them, there was always that loving hand, promising that one day things would be different and he would restore his children in love. It is something God yearns to do. There is a lovely image of this in Hosea:

> How can I give you up, Ephraim? How can I hand you over, Israel? How can I treat you like Admah? How can I make you like Zeboiim? My heart is changed within me; all my compassion is aroused. (Hosea 11:8)

In the book of Hosea, God has sent several warnings about judgement and harsh treatment which will reduce Israel to the pitiful state of the cities around Sodom and Gomorrah (Admah and Zeboiim were two other cities on the plain near Sodom as mentioned in Genesis 10:19). You can see from the verse above that it almost breaks God's heart to be so harsh, and he longs to show love and forgiveness to his children instead. You can feel the anguish in his heart.

Jeremiah also teaches this same aspect of God's love:

> 'How gladly would I treat you like sons and give you a desirable land, the most beautiful inheritance of any nation.' I thought you would call me 'Father' and not turn away from following me. (Jeremiah 3:19)

It can be difficult to accept something from someone you love, because you know how much it costs them to provide it, and they are doing so only because of their love for you. Such love is humbling. The love God demonstrates is a sacrificial love, where God gives us everything (for example, Romans 5:8), and it is completely unconditional. A love earned is easy to accept, but one undeserved is much harder. In fact, this is one of the biggest obstacles to the gospel for many people.

A child has no difficulty with this though, and daily welcomes the love of his parents and peers without questioning it. There is never any doubt in a child's mind about receiving an ice cream from a parent on a hot (or even cold) day. They never stop to think, 'Daddy bought me one yesterday, and so I have to buy him one today.' They receive a free gift gladly, without rejecting it. This is the love that God is looking for adults to accept, and which we are often too sophisticated to enjoy. It is a love we can and should be extending to each other, and learning to receive from both God and each other. For most of us, the first part is the easier of the two.

There is no doubt that God loves us, but our view of love sometimes gets too woolly. He loves us truly, and in a powerful way. God as father loves his children with a perfect love.

*(iii) Mercy* Having mercy on someone deserving punishment is a great sign of love. Again it is something seen in family relationships, where the family 'closes ranks' to protect one of its own. We even have a saying for it: 'blood is thicker than water'. It means protecting the person, regardless of what they have done, because they are family and loved. Similarly, love is God's motivation to show mercy repeatedly to Israel over the centuries. The psalmist puts it like this: 'As a father has compassion on his children, so the LORD has compassion on those who fear him' (Psalm 103:13).

Mercy knows no limits either. God is always prepared to withhold punishment from those who repent. He is ready to show forgiveness for the hundredth time (Matthew 18:22), and love for the hundredth time. He is not a God who loses patience. Any parent will know what it is like to have to tell a child off constantly for making the same mistake time after time. Any teacher will know how difficult it is to love a child who will simply not listen and who keeps making the same error over and over again. It is only the best teacher, or the most loving parent, that can patiently, lovingly and forgivingly listen once again to the child who does this. This is a picture of how God operates.

God has dealt with Israel like this through the centuries. Time and time again he warns them about their behaviour through the prophets (for example, Amos 2:11–12), yet Israel ignored God repeatedly. God did not stop loving and showing mercy for an amazing length of time. His love for his children is vast and gracious, going far beyond our own capacity for forgiveness to each other. Even when he shows judgement, it is always balanced by mercy. The punishment God sends often has an element of teaching in it, which encourages the people to call out to God again. When they do, God is always eager to respond in mercy.

*(iv) Encouraging faith and growth*     God leads and develops the history of Israel in careful ways. His children are placed in certain situations so that they will cry out to him (see Job 35:9). The first half of the book of Judges amply illustrates this. Time and time again, Israel forgets God, and so he allows raiding nations to worry Israel and make them remember to pray to him. When they do, God sends a deliverer (Judge/Saviour) to them, who rescues them, and encourages their faith in him once more.[2] God's plan has always been to further Israel's growth in understanding and maturity. He has always worked in ways that would encourage them to trust him more. He is a father whose aim is to train his children and stretch them in ways that will benefit them without breaking them. It is a demanding role, but important in parenting. God is arranging all of human

2   Judges 3:7–11 is a simple and small example of this cycle which is
    repeated throughout the first half of the book.

history for this purpose. The growth and development of his children is that important to him.

Even the Garden of Eden was illustrative of this. He placed Adam in a perfect environment where he had all he needed. There was safety, companionship, food, work and fellowship with God, but there were also challenges and commands.[3] The purpose here was to stretch and encourage Adam's love and willing obedience to God. It was not to condemn him. God has a tender heart, a nurturing heart for his children. He wanted Adam and Eve to grow in their knowledge and experience with him.

This is an area that parents can know to be particularly frustrating and irritating. Allowing a child to help us in jobs we are doing can be a real treat for them, as well as good for their development, but the jobs take twice as long and make twice as much mess. For the older children, this takes the form of letting them go, trusting things will be all right, allowing them to make their mistakes and learn from them. It can be nerve-wracking indeed. Yet it is necessary, as God knows and has perfected in his care for his children.

*(v) Taking responsibility for the children*    Here is a difficult thought. God is willing to accept the responsibility for his people. In the New Testament, we see that Christ demonstrates this when he takes our sins upon himself on the cross. In the Old Testament, we see God being examined by the nations. They judge God by the way his children behave. God has linked his name and honour to Israel's (Jeremiah 34:16). When Israel behaves in a way that is disgraceful, it reflects on God. Similarly, the behaviour of the child reflects on the

---

3  Adam's relationship with God is defined in Genesis 2.

parent. That is something the New Testament also understands when it commands that elders should have children
that are a credit to the parent: 'An elder must be . . . a man
whose children believe and are not open to the charge of
being wild and disobedient' (Titus 1:6). Are we really ready to
say we can be judged by the way the children in our care
behave? God was.

Conversely it also relates to the fact that God cannot allow
his children to struggle unnecessarily. He cannot have the
world looking at his people and thinking he is not much of a
God. He is honour-bound to care and provide (Psalm 25:3).
If the children in our care are to see God, then they need to
experience for themselves the joy of seeing God meet their
needs personally, as well as corporately as a family.

We can see this same attitude worked out as God tells his
people to care for the orphans and fatherless.[4] As Israel must
take responsibility for caring for the weak in their community,
an Israelite parent is also to show a social awareness and care.
It is not enough to see God at work in the family; the child
needs to see God working through the family (including
themselves) to the needs around them.

*Summary*    From these attributes of God, and the way he has
dealt with Israel in the past, we can see that God is
committed to the care and nourishment of his own children,
and as such holds up a perfect model of fatherhood for us to
follow. The very name 'the children of Israel' shows a caring,
protecting, nourishing hand to those he has chosen.

In so far as the people of Israel were God's children, we can

---

4  Deuteronomy 14:29 is one of 39 similar references to the care of the
   fatherless in the Old Testament.

have no hesitation in saying that God loves his children and is particularly concerned about their nurture and care. What is more, he holds out a marvellous picture and model of parenthood for us to follow.

## (b) God as mother

In case any mothers are sitting back comfortably reading this, smug in the knowledge that their husbands are being exposed here, and thinking that this is all going to be another male-dominated book, beware. The image God portrays for us in the Bible is not only that of the father. It is much more politically correct than that. The image of God includes that of a mother as well. However, there is no intimation that God is feminine from this picture, any more than 'God is male' could have been inferred from the previous section. God is only described in human terms for our convenience. He is Spirit and Truth. Nevertheless, he does demonstrate some of what we term as the 'softer' and 'warmer' characteristics that we associate with the perfect mother.

*(i) God the protector*   Psalm 17:8, for example, has the lovely picture of God being protective and sheltering the psalmist in the shadow of his wings. The natural parenting instinct to protect and shelter is a gift from God. God himself extends that same attitude towards us as his children. In its softest form, the phrase 'give me a cuddle' does have meaning in relation to God. In some of our better moments, when we are feeling close to him, we are certainly being 'cuddled' by him.

On a harder note, the idea of God as a mother bear[5] also has relevance. An angry mother is almost legendary as a thing

---

5   2 Kings 2:24 suggests the anger of a she-bear.

to fear. In the way that God feels protective about his children, and angry against those that seek to harm them, this picture makes us feel very safe in God's hands. Children look for these things in their mothers.

*(ii) God the midwife*   Alternatively, in Psalm 22:9, we have the picture of God as midwife bringing the baby to birth. We are reminded of the skilled care and protection as well as the sense of relief the midwife brings as she arrives to sort out the complications of the pregnancy. The parents may have been desperately worried, but now the midwife is here the whole problem will soon be over. In the same way, God makes possible that which could not happen otherwise, and we can relax as he takes control.

It is also an intimate picture. Childbirth is an undignified, private and precious moment. The parents are frazzled and worn out, perhaps feeling open and vulnerable. God is involved with the messy parts of our lives, and helps in the areas we cannot share with others, as they are too private or painful. God is a tender healer and helper; not at all like the nuisance friend who comes stomping in, loud voiced and insensitive. A high calling for parents once more, particularly as children suffer and struggle in their emotional development, is to keep lines of communication and trust going where other approaches may well lead to disaster.

*(iii) God the wet nurse*   In Isaiah 49:15 we see how God's love surpasses even that of a mother suckling her baby. Here the image is that of tenderness and nourishment. Once again it is an intimate picture. Psychologists speak of the importance of this 'bonding' time, where mother and baby form the basis of their relationship. God wants to cuddle and hold us, while feeding us. He wants us to lean back, relax, and

surrender to him, stop our crying and draw from him. Again, this is something we find difficult as adults, but which a child can cope with much more readily.

*(iv) God the comforter*    Isaiah 66:13 compares God's love to that of a mother comforting the children of Israel. The image of a child with a hurt knee coming running to Mummy for a plaster and a cuddle is irresistible here. Plasters or cuddles do not reduce the pain (in fact the washing prior to the plaster can be very painful indeed), but Mummy knows about the problem now, and has made it better. That is what matters. The child soon stops the tears and, pain forgotten, is off again. Our churches would be a lot healthier mentally if we could only lean on God like this.

*Summary*    All these images show the love and care of God in a way that is very much more tender than could come from a masculine image. Yet it is a true quality of God in relation to his people, and one the church needs to take on board. It is necessary for our children to feel this security from their parents. Once again God shows us the perfect role model.

*Conclusion*

We can be certain that God cares for his children with a perfect love, encompassing all we see that is best in parenthood. It is perfectly illustrated for us by God's care for his children, Israel.

## 2. God has a heart for children

Jesus said, 'I praise you, Father, Lord of heaven and earth, because you have hidden these things from the wise and learned, and revealed them to little children.' (Matthew 11:25)

Our second theme explores God's special concern for children. In the Old Testament we will see that he is prepared to focus on them and their needs.

### (a) God cares for the weak

Throughout Scripture, we see God taking the part of the weak and the defenceless, the widow and the orphan. The young child particularly fits into this category, and therefore can be considered to be under the protection of God in the same way as widows and orphans.

The child in ancient near-eastern cultures was really only seen as a possession and was often sacrificed for the benefit of the family. This would have been especially true in Canaanite culture, where children were offered to the gods, for example to the Moabite god Chemosh (2 Kings 3:27), and to the Ammonite god Molech (1 Kings 11:7). The Bible specifically forbids this practice as abominable (Leviticus 18:21). Children are more than possessions for parents to bribe the gods with. They are a special gift from God, to be loved, nurtured and trained.

Then the Bible goes further and commands that the orphan and the widow be granted care and favour (Deuteronomy 24:19–21). As a result of God's concern for justice, he inevitably has a special place for them in his heart. In our society particularly, when there are so many children without both parents for whatever reason, God's heart must often be breaking. As within almost every society, children are the most vulnerable members.

Children with physical, mental or social difficulties can sometimes appear disruptive and cause us to back away from them. God's reaction is the precise opposite. This is an indirect form of love that God has for children. There are now more direct ideas to be considered.

## (b) Importance of children in God's plan

*(i) God can use children*   He sometimes delights to do so. At times, God has chosen children specifically, to speak through them, and even to bring words of judgement upon adults. This applies even to infants, as the psalmist puts it: 'From the lips of children and infants you have ordained praise because of your enemies, to silence the foe and the avenger' (Psalm 8:2).

Jesus uses this psalm to devastating effect in the New Testament, when the Pharisees and priests refuse to praise him but the children will (Matthew 21:15–16). He shows that the leaders are opposing God, while the children can see God more clearly than the priests can. Children can have an attitude to God that is better than all our religious theology. He uses the simple and weak to shame the proud.

Sometimes we are too proud, or sophisticated, or complicated for God to speak to us, and so he will employ a child, for example when God spoke to Eli through Samuel the boy servant (1 Samuel 3:1–17). He may use a child to speak to us as well, especially if we are too busy or too proud to listen to God for ourselves.

*(ii) The word Na'ar*   Among the different words that Hebrew has for child, there is a word used regularly in the Old Testament that is a bit unusual. It is regularly translated as 'teenager' or 'youth', and carries with it the idea of servant. This can be a literal servant, as for example in its use in Numbers 22:22. Here the word seems to suggest more the fact that 'they serve' than the idea of childhood.

Yet the word also carries with it the idea of a 'lack of maturity' that characterises a child. In Jewish society when people could be married by the age of fifteen, the concept of 'teenager' does not really occur. Therefore the word probably refers to young people from eight years old up to puberty. In that society (as in many others too) they would have been working right through this stage.

The word then has two facets to its meaning. One suggests pre-pubescent age; the other suggests useful service given.

However, occasionally the same word is also translated as 'infant'. Yet even here the meaning has to relate to the servant rather than the age aspect of the word. It is only used for particular babies who are already marked out as a servant of God by a prophecy or some other event. This word is used of Ishmael (Genesis 21:17), Moses (Exodus 2:6), Samson (Judges 13:7), Samuel (1 Samuel 1:22) and Jeremiah (Jeremiah 1:7), and it seems to suggest that God is willing to use the infant when he is capable of service. In fact we know from some examples that God even has plans for the adult from before birth: 'Before I formed you in the womb I knew you, before you were born I set you apart; I appointed you as a prophet to the nations' (Jeremiah 1:5).

The prime example of this is Samuel. His parents were having difficulty having children, something that regularly seems to be of significance in God's purposes in the Bible. On this occasion, Hannah had promised God that Samuel her son would serve in the temple at Shiloh when he was old enough to leave his mother's side. This happened after he was weaned, which would have been around the age of two or three (somewhat later than in our society). It was in the temple that God spoke to him, a young boy, in preference to the high priest of the day, Eli. God chose a child to speak out an important prophecy at a crucial time in Israel's history. *Theophanies* (God physically revealing himself – here through the voice calling to Samuel) were rare in the Old Testament, yet here we have one given to a mere child. God did not consider him a *mere child,* but his servant. Based on 1 Samuel 3:7, it is even possible that this is the child's own conversion narrative. However, it is probably better to match it to the calling of Isaiah (Isaiah 6), or Jeremiah (Jeremiah 1), as Samuel's calling to the prophetic office, a work he was to carry on for many years. Such a call is amazing enough, but it is incredible when you consider that Eli, God's longstanding servant, was asleep just down the hall, and heard nothing. Experienced and mature believers were available, yet God chose a child.

*Summary*    The Hebrew word *Na'ar* suggests 'servanthood'. It can be used instead of another word meaning 'called and chosen to serve God'. If God is prepared to use selected children and infants as his special servants, then so should we. It speaks highly of God's view of children.

### (c) The 'seed'

Ever since Genesis, Israel had been expecting a child to come, through whom the whole world would be blessed. That child never came in a way that they recognised, though Israel was looking for him by the title of 'Messiah'. This idea of a 'seed' came to be something of a symbol for them as they waited. Parents are always enthusiastic about the values of their children anyway, but in this case there was a genuine prophetic reason for expectation. Abraham battled with childlessness for a long time, waiting for the promised child, which did not come until he was practically speaking too old to have children. Abraham and Sarah, who received the promise of children so personally, simply had to wait and trust God for many years. God used the expectation to teach them faith and patience (and a great many other lessons too). It gave the Israelites reason to value their children and allow them to serve God from an early age. Their child could be 'the seed'.

Judah's daughter-in-law, Tamar, had a similar disappointment. She was desperately waiting for a child (Genesis 38) but was being denied one. Eventually this child was born, and named Perez. Ruth also struggles to have a son to continue the family line. Eventually, through Boaz, she does, and the village leaders of the day then pray that her child will be like a line of Perez (Ruth 4:12). Perez as a baby then stands for the child given by God who will continue the work of God in his generation. Perez came to represent the child that finally was born as a result of God's plan, even despite difficulty, and became a real blessing and future hope for the family concerned. While the sign of Perez was a special event for the chosen 'seed' line, it does demonstrate the way the people felt about children. From the very beginning of the revelation of God, the birth of a child can be seen to have divine implications.[6]

So God is certainly a God who delights to use children in his work. Church history is also full of times when God uses children.[7] Children should therefore be part of the plans of our churches, as well as our families.

### 3. Children are a blessing from the Lord

'Sons are a heritage from the LORD, children a reward from him' (Psalm 127:3). God's gift of children to parents is a special occasion today, but it was even more so in the time of the ancient world.

---

6  G. Dallow, 'Children BC' in *Children's Ministry* magazine, Issue 5, 1999.

7  See Harry Sprange, *Kingdom Kids* (Christian Focus, 1994).

*(a) They were essential for the fulfilment of the creation mandate (Genesis 1:28)*

Adam and Eve gave their son Cain a name that means 'brought forth with the help of the Lord' (Genesis 4:1). God had commanded that they should have children (Genesis 1:28), and they were trying to fulfil the command.

So the arrival of a child was not merely part of a natural process but it was God's special gift. When children came, parents rejoiced – not just at seeing a new life, but in receiving a token of God's blessing (Psalm 127:3).[8]

*(b) They were essential for the continuance of the covenant with God*

God had made a covenant with his people, and if his people were to be faithful to his covenant, then they must become a great nation, as many as the stars in the sky (Genesis 15:5). Whether they were good, godly or bad was not the primary issue, but simply that they were there: they were essential for the family, clan, tribe and nation. This concern was not merely nationalistic; it was deeply religious. The growth and development of the nation of Israel, God's covenant people, required children and a future.[9] The male had to be circumcised and accepted into the covenant community because of his birth. It branded the covenant into the sex organs of the newly born son. It signified that he was entering this covenant, and that he would eventually bequeath it to his own children. This is why, when Israelites had children, they rejoiced, not just because the human race would continue and their names endure but because God's covenant would go

---

8    Eric Lane, *Special Children?* (Grace Publications, 1996), p.11.
9    *Ibid.*

on.[10] Childbearing thus became one of the blessings associated with covenant obedience (Deuteronomy 28:1–4).

*(c) They were essential for the perpetuation of the family name*

The arrival of an heir was one of the most important events for an Israelite; his name and line must continue. It was considered as important as we might consider eternity to be.[11] This attitude appears particularly in the case of the Levirite marriage, where family members had responsibility to have sex with recent childless widows, in order that the family branch would continue (Deuteronomy 25:5–6). The peculiar story of Ruth and Boaz becomes clearer once this principle is established. It also explains some of God's more bloodthirsty pronouncements, e.g. Isaiah 14:21. (The way to destroy a nation was not to defeat them in battle, but to kill their children. This was what Pharaoh had tried to do in Exodus 1.) It is also the reason why families preferred male babies to female, for the males ensured the perpetuation of the family name.

The idea of continuance was always very important to the Israelites. It was generally considered that a family that could not have children was under a curse, because they would soon die out and lose their place in God's family.

An Israelite's view of eternity seemed to depend a lot on the idea that their children, and their children's children, would be there. The children would continue to farm the land after they had gone, and their bones would remain in the burial site, with successive generations following them. So the

10 *Ibid.*, pp.14–15.
11 *Ibid.*, p.12.

gift of a child meant that the line would continue, the dynasty would go on.

> . . . so that your days and the days of your children may be many in the land that the LORD swore to give your forefathers, as many as the days that the heavens are above the earth. (Deuteronomy 11:21)

## (d) They belong to God

The place of the firstborn makes this clear. Ever since the first Passover festival, the Jews have set apart the firstborn children for God because they belonged to God. If it had not been for God's provision at the Passover, they would have died (Exodus 12:23). As they belong to God in this literal and technical sense, from the Passover onwards Israel had to offer a sacrifice to redeem their firstborn sons back from God so they could look after them. This was true of the animals too. The animals also belonged to God, but Israel was commanded to use them as sacrifices. Thankfully, this did not relate to the firstborn son. This is what God was showing Abraham (among other things) when God commanded that he should sacrifice Isaac (Genesis 22:1–14).

## (e) They are a gift from God

Having children was not something that Israel considered an automatic right. Children were the future, and the continuation of the families' inheritance. A wife that could bear children was an important asset for a family, especially one that could bear sons. These days we know it is actually the father's sperm that determines the sex of the child, so this evaluation of a wife was very unfair. Genesis sums up the urgency of needing to bear children: 'When Rachel saw that she was not bearing Jacob any children, she became jealous of her sister. So she said to Jacob, "Give me children, or I'll die!"' (Genesis 30:1).[12]

So the birth of particularly a male child was a very important event, and there were great celebrations surrounding it. In 1 Samuel 1:24–28 we read of the celebrations Hannah gave at the birth of Samuel.[13] When a son was born, he was placed immediately on his father's knees (Genesis 50:23; Job 3:12). The psalmist's words, 'From birth I was cast upon you; from my mother's womb you have been my God' (Psalm 22:10) describe the father receiving his new son and signify God's care from the moment of birth.

### (f) Barrenness – a curse

The loss of children, or barrenness, was often considered to be a judgement. This is illustrated in Leviticus 26:22:

> I will send wild animals against you, and they will rob you of your children, destroy your cattle and make you so few in number that your roads will be deserted. (See also Genesis 20:17; Numbers 3:4; Psalm 58:8; Hosea 9:14)

Most people have a soft spot for children and do not like to see them being hurt. For Israel it was even more significant because of this idea of family continuance. However, the lack of God's gift of children was not always for the purposes of judgement. Sarah's difficulty in conceiving was clearly there so that God could use it to encourage the faith of the couple, and make them live out a life of faith.

In many instances this curse could have been removed by

---

12 Other references would include Psalm 127:3 or Psalm 128:3.
13 See also Ruth 4:13–14; Jeremiah 20:15.

God and turned into a blessing instead, if the people had either demonstrated repentance or the purpose of their barrenness was completed (as in the case of Hannah, or Sarah). The psalmist says: 'He settles the barren woman in her home as a happy mother of children. Praise the LORD' (Psalm 113:9).

## Conclusion

God sees children as a blessing and a necessary part of the human existence. Without children, Israelite society would have been bereft and cursed. The church, therefore, must have a similar view. Practically, as well as theologically, we know this is true. Any church without a thriving work among children will be struggling within 15 years, and practically closed within 30.

In conclusion, we can be sure that God has a heart for children. He holds out to us the perfect pattern of fatherhood, caring for his people Israel. He also shows throughout the Bible that he is prepared to use children just as they are. In short, God cares for children more than we realise or might be prepared to admit.

# 2

# *At What Age Is a Child in Need of Salvation?*

After thinking about the special place that God has in his heart for children, we now need to ask whether children need salvation or not. If God feels so warmly about children, will he allow them into heaven anyway; or do they need saving? We saw in the last chapter that God has a heart for the orphan and the fatherless in particular, so is it possible that the younger children are and the more in need of protection, the less likely they are to actually need salvation at all?

This is a controversial question that makes emotions run high in debate or counselling. It would be very cruel to tell the parents of a dead child that there is no hope of their child being in heaven. Perhaps because of the emotions inherent within the issue, or perhaps because the Bible appears silent on this point, there are several positions that we need to consider carefully before answering this difficult issue.

The whole debate is also going to revolve around the issue of hell. That is because this is the clearest and most stark issue in relation to salvation. It is not true to say that the only reason a child (or adult) has to become a Christian is to avoid hell. Salvation is much more to do with a foundation for growing and developing into a beautiful child of God. Sanctification is a process, and not as stark an issue as hell, but hell will have to be the difficult issue we focus on.

## 1. Innocent until proven guilty

'If you were blind, you would not be guilty of sin; but now that you claim to see, your guilt remains' (John 9:41). This is a popular position, and suggests that all children belong to Christ until they deliberately reject him. This means that if a child died before developing a conscious reasoning ability, the child would count as being innocent and God would accept them into heaven. This is a very comfortable position, and emotionally has a lot going for it. It suggests that a child who is unable to make a choice at all because he is too young, cannot have chosen darkness, or evil, and therefore still belongs to God, as an unspoilt creation. They are 'innocent until proven guilty'.

This is based on the idea that God is a God of love and mercy, who does not act in a harsh and unforgiving manner, nor condemn people unnecessarily to hell. He will not hold guilty those who have had no chance to respond to God, and they are not under the power of the second death (eternal judgement). Hell is a place reserved for those who have deliberately rejected Christ, those who have loved darkness instead of light.[1] This means that those who have not loved darkness rather than light, who have not deliberately rejected Christ, are still included. Is this what Jesus meant when he said, 'Let the *little* children come to me . . . for the kingdom of heaven belongs to such as these' (Matthew 19:14)? If this is right,

---

1   John Inchley, *The Realities of Childhood* (Scripture Union, 1985), p. 111.

then we all start as innocents, in the same way as Adam, but sadly, given enough time, we all seem able to prove ourselves sinners by practice, as Adam once did. This idea has even given rise to the maxim 'Give a man enough rope, and he will hang himself'. All this is without doubt, but the crucial part of this argument is that we start off in life as innocent, and then wreck it for ourselves. There are some issues that arise out of this position, which need examining.

## (a) Original sin

The orthodox doctrine of original sin teaches that mankind is born in sin and is cut off from God. This means that a child, even at birth, is a sinner in need of salvation, and if the child dies immediately after birth, it will go to hell as a sinner. The church has agreed with the doctrine of original sin ever since a major discussion rocked the church in the fourth century AD. Pelagius, one of the main players in the debate, believed that:

> Adam's descendants . . . are born innocent as Adam was before his fall; in so far as they are sinners it is not because they have inherited a sinful tendency from him, but because they have followed in his footsteps of their own free choice.[2]

Pelagius's position is very similar to the position of 'innocent until proven guilty'. However, after a long debate particularly with Augustine, the church condemned Pelagius and this position as heretical. It has held that view ever since, and preferred Augustine's doctrine of original sin. To be clear about what we mean, we need a definition for original sin.

---

2   F. F. Bruce, *The Spreading Flame* (Paternoster Press, 1958), p. 335.

> Since humanity's fall, everyone inherits an inclination to sin and a desire to go his or her own way rather than to obey God. Human beings are sinful by nature. There is no need to teach a child to do wrong; it comes naturally to everyone.[3]

The church applied the idea of children needing salvation to specific teachings about the need to save and baptise them. Origen, who lived from AD 185 to 254, wrote about this, and required children to be baptised to be rid of the 'uncleanness' (he cannot bring himself to say 'sin') which attaches to everyone who is born.[4]

Augustine,[5] as Pelagius's opponent, obviously believed in original sin, by which he meant 'a conviction that each human being is born, not only with an inborn tendency to turn away from God (which all Christian thinkers had agreed was the case), but also already guilty of sin'.

If Origen and Augustine were right, then a newly born baby will go to hell if it dies. This is a very harsh statement, and will probably have already caused revulsion in you as a reader.

## (b) Only potentially guilty?

Some modern theologians, for example Ron Buckland in *Children and God*, or John Inchley, have attempted to soften the statements made above. They suggest that original sin is not a court ruling already made against humanity. It is merely a potentiality, a leaning, and an in-built desire within people. It is not until an individual wilfully acts upon it that it comes into effect. Original sin therefore becomes a sort of threat for

---

3  Lion CD of the Bible and Christianity v 2.0.
4  W. A. Strange, *Children in the Early Church* (Paternoster Press, 1996), p. 89.
5  *Ibid.*, p. 95.

the future . . . a spiritual sort of 'wait until your father gets home'. It is not a reality at birth.

Other theologians, for example M. J. Erickson, have taken this further, questioning whether children really are guilty and accountable in the same sense as adults. This is a radical idea, and seems to imply that God judges infants differently from the way in which he judges the adult population. It talks not of 'original sin', but of the 'age of responsibility' before which the child is not guilty.

Original sin in this newer definition[6] means that we receive a corrupt nature, but we are not at this point guilty. The individual has to deliberately choose right or wrong for themselves when they reach an age where they can understand the issues involved. Until they do, they cannot be held guilty. This means that children cannot be found guilty until they reach the age of responsibility.[7]

This is a very different definition from the one we looked at a moment ago. While we might agree with this emotionally, defending this scripturally is very difficult. Changing our theology to fit with our experiences, or wishes, rather than with the Bible, is inherently dangerous. Adopting this position leaves us saying that a child can carry on doing whatever he likes, but until he reaches a certain age, he cannot be found guilty. This of course is what our legal system suggests, and gives rise to the difficulties we have with juvenile crime. It seems to enshrine some of the problems many recognise with the legal system today and thus could be a recommendation against accepting it as a theology, on the basis that it does not seem to be working in society. The definition cannot be

---

6  M. J. Erickson, *Christian Theology* (Baker, 1987), p. 639.
7  *Ibid.*

defended on biblical grounds, nor can it be defended on pragmatic grounds.

From a theological perspective, this has a further problem.
This position suggests that when a child is born, he is born
into a situation of conditional guilt (conditional on the child
actually doing something wrong one day), not actual guilt.
This position further means that whatever wrongs an infant
does are unimportant, until they are old enough to choose to
rebel personally. Yet there is no mention of conditional guilt
in the Bible, and it is difficult to work out from the Bible as a
doctrine. Does God record the infant's sins, but only in pencil
as it were, because they are not yet important? They may
become important if the child chooses to rebel against God.
Such an idea is a mockery of sin. Either God is offended by
rebellion, and will punish it, or he is willing to forgive it, as
far as the east is from the west. There appears to be no other
option for God from the Bible.

## (c) Can we redefine original sin?

Is original sin actually biblical? Some theologians dismiss it[8]
by claiming that it is Augustinian rather than Pauline, and
therefore reflects later theological thinking rather than true
biblical doctrine. So rather than discuss the question of original sin, we need to consider the question of when children
choose to sin as Adam did.

However, this ignores certain crucial aspects of the biblical
revelation. The Bible makes it clear that Adam's sin brings
ruin to the world, and to all people: see, for example, Romans
8:20 and 1 Corinthians 15:22. The Bible teaches about the
imputed guilt of original sin, for example in 1 Corinthians
15:22. Changing the question is therefore running away from

---

8   Ron Buckland, *Children and God* (Scripture Union, 1938), p. 29.

the significance of the theology of original sin, which means that the person is guilty by association with Adam. Merely being 'born of a woman' is enough to condemn you to hell.

Changing the question leads as we have seen to a happy conclusion, one that is morally easy to accept. However, it has to be considered with suspicion because it side-steps the issues which really lie behind the definition of original sin. It becomes a man-centred debate focusing on the way that children choose sin, rather than the traditional theological idea, which focuses on the in-built guilt of each member of the human race at conception. In the standard interpretation of original sin, people start off life guilty.[9]

Some might argue that original sin is a theological rather than a biblical concept. This is a poor accusation. Theology has to arise from a biblical position, or it is not biblical theology. Theology should merely attempt to systematise biblical verses, making clear the positions that individual verses are teaching, and how they fit together into a system. Ever since the debate in the fourth century, the church has recognised that the doctrine is one such teaching, even though it is not mentioned by that name in the Bible. If we were to follow this sort of argument, we could also dismiss the doctrine of the Trinity, which does not appear as a word anywhere in the Bible. However, it is a fundamental belief of the Christian faith, and an abandonment of it marks a person's slide into heresy. It is not an acceptable argument therefore to say that the doctrine of original sin is a theological rather than a biblical position, any more than it is to say it of the Trinity.

Perhaps the problem is the increase in experienced-based

---

9 W. Grudem, *Systematic Theology: An Introduction to Biblical Doctrine* (IVP, 1994), p. 495.

theology rather than biblical theology, which has, as we have already noticed, given rise to this whole debate by wanting to remove an awkward doctrine.

While the logic of this redefinition of original sin appears to fit badly with the biblical doctrine, historically some very reputable groups and theologians have supported it. The Baptist Union confession in 1677 appears to support it by accepting the idea that dying children could be considered as going to heaven. Spurgeon also clearly supported this idea when in a letter of 1869 he wrote:

> I have never at any time in my life said, believed or imagined that any infants under any circumstances would be cast into hell. I have always believed in the salvation of all infants ... I do not believe that on this earth there is a single professing Christian holding the damnation of infants; or if there be he must be insane or utterly ignorant of Christianity.[10]

These are strong words from a famous and highly respected Christian. There are also many well-known theologians today who would be happy with the same position.[11] While this is a pleasant and popular thought, we have to measure it against our authority, the Bible. Perhaps one important question to ask is 'On what basis are they saved?'

The whole of biblical revelation insists that it cannot be on their own merits, or on the basis of their own righteousness or innocence, but it must be entirely on the basis of Christ's redemptive work and regeneration of the Holy Spirit within them.[12] Yet this position adds another possibility. If they are

---

10 Quoted by Eric Lane, *Special Children?*, p. 59.
11 W. Hendrickson, *The Bible in the Life Hereafter* (Baker, 1959), p.101, quotes Hodge Warfield and Boettner.
12 W. Grudem, *Systematic Theology*, p. 500.

too young to have reached the age of accountability, then can they also be saved? From a biblical perspective, there have to be serious questions over any attempt to remove the judicial guilt that the newly born already have.

*Summary* The arguments that theologians put forward in support of a redefinition appear to be based on a view of the love of God, and the idea that God will not condemn innocent children to hell without the chance of repentance. The difficulty is that this is an emotional response, not a theological one, and it focuses on one aspect of the character of God alone: his love. Admittedly it is not simply a position of sentimentalism, but then it does not arise directly from Scripture either. It clashes with the standard and traditional theological view of original sin. It suggests that original sin is merely a potential condition and that it alone is insufficient to condemn us to separation from God. While in the Bible this does not arise in the context of children particularly, its implication is clear, and a powerful argument. We have to be suspicious of the motivation for this position because the trends in current thinking have moved from a theological to a pragmatic approach. We are asked to begin with what children can 'feel' and 'experience', not from biblical teaching.[13]

This has to be a retrograde step. Theology should interpret our experience not arise from our experience. We should go to the Bible for our belief, and then apply it to our lives regardless of how painful that might be. God will act in a just manner, because it is his nature.

---

13 Eric Lane, *Special Children?*, p. 48.

## 2. Children of Christians are saved until they sin for themselves

'I will establish my covenant as an everlasting covenant between me and you and your descendants after you' (Genesis 17:7). This is a subtle variation of position, which suggests that the children of believing parents, though guilty because of original sin, initially belong to God by virtue of their parentage. The parents are in a covenant agreement with God, and that also covers the children until they are old enough to make their own choices. Some people have been bold enough to say that the presence of at least one Christian parent cancels out the consequences of a child's sinful nature.[14] This is on the basis of the understanding of a passage in 1 Corinthians: 'Otherwise your children would be unclean, but as it is, they are holy' (1 Corinthians 7:14).

This is quite a popular opinion among evangelical and particularly reformed commentators. They see the children of believers as included in the covenant between God and his people and therefore as having a place in the church.[15] This salvation is based on the faith of the parent, and some covenantal theology. If the parent is in covenant with God then the child by default remains within it until they deliberately abandon it personally. Again, as with the above position, this one also has a lot of theological respectability. The synod of Dort in 1615, the Savoy declaration of the Congregational churches in 1658 and also the Westminster Confession all support this idea.

### (a) Scriptural evidence

With regard to 1 Corinthians 7:14, the theology there is difficult, and does not really discuss the salvational state of

14 Ron Buckland, *Children and God* (Scripture Union, 1938), p. 31.
15 Eric Lane, *Special Children?*, p. 46.

infants at all. We can say this for several reasons.

First, the theme of the passage is to do with divorce, and theologians disagree even about what it really means in its clear context. It does not really relate to a discussion on infant salvation at all. It is always unwise to draw a theology from a single verse when that verse is unclear anyway. It is doubly dangerous to do so when the context is clearly talking about something else.

Second, even assuming that the verse really was able to teach us on this issue, there is nothing in the verse or its context that helps us define an age of innocence for these children. From this verse, the argument applies to infants or eight-year-olds equally well. If the verse really were to teach that the child was saved by the faith of the parent, it would be any child, until they stopped being a child. In fact, if there is a point about the age of the child in the passage, the Greek word used there is *tekna,* which usually denotes older children, rather than *paidia*, which is regularly used for younger ones who could otherwise be described as innocents.

Third, if the passage is really talking about salvation for the one person on the basis of the faith of the other, then its primary application would be to suggest that the unsaved husband (or wife) of the saved partner would also be saved due to their partner's faith. This is unacceptable theology, and no one would attempt to defend that from this verse. Similarly, teaching that an infant can be saved on the basis of a parent's faith is unacceptable from this verse.

Another, and much more reasonable, argument develops from 2 Samuel 12:23, speaking of the death of David and Bathsheba's son. David says, 'I will go to him, but he will not return to me.' It suggests that David knew his son was in heaven, where David would one day go. His son was only seven days old (verse 18), and therefore David clearly expected his child to be saved on the basis either of innocence or David's covenant with God. He was therefore as content as possible given the death of his son, and able to continue with life secure in the knowledge that his son was in heaven. We can go further than this, because the child was not circumcised, and therefore could not be saved under any covenantal agreement. We can be certain of this because in Israelite law children were not circumcised until the eighth day, and only then if healthy. Therefore David's expectation of seeing his son again has to be based on the child's innocence.

However, this understanding requires a New Testament interpretation, where heaven is for those who trust in Jesus, and hell is for the sinners who do not. The Old Testament concept of life after death was rather more basic, and cloudier than this. They believed in an afterlife in Sheol (the most frequently used Hebrew word for the place after death), but Sheol related to the abode of both the righteous and the unrighteous dead (Psalm 9:17) or the place of the wicked (Jonah 2:2). It refers simply to the abode of the dead. Therefore David's expectations about where his son will go after death do not really help here. He merely expects that his son is in Sheol along with all the other dead. The only way we could suggest that David expects his child to be in heaven is to suggest that, in the Old Testament view of Sheol, the righteous could not see the unrighteous in death. However, this is something that the New Testament passage (showing the flavour of Old Testament understanding) in Luke 16:19–31 of the rich man and Lazarus rejects.

Following the Old Testament view of death through, David's covenant theology[16] will only allow us to suggest that

---

16 J. Honeycott, 'The Child within the Old Testament Community', in *Children and Conversion* (Broadman, 1970), p. 22.

David is accepting the child's death. David knows that the child cannot return to him from death, but that he will one day follow his son down the same path into death.

However, if we do accept this idea, we still have the problem of David's acceptance and ceasing to mourn. His advisors on hearing of the child's death fear David will do something silly (2 Samuel 12:18) whereas David acts in the opposite way, picks himself up, and gets on with life. The advisors cannot understand his actions and they do look odd. Why is the child's death a reason not to fast and weep? David was apparently mourning before (verse 17) but not now (verse 21), and they cannot understand the mentality that ceases to do this when the child dies. David gives his answer when he says in verses 22 and 23:

> While the child was still alive, I fasted and wept. I thought, 'Who knows? The LORD may be gracious to me and let the child live.' But now that he is dead, why should I fast? Can I bring him back again? I will go to him, but he will not return to me. (2 Samuel 12:22–23)

David is showing a completely different and very healthy attitude towards death from that of his advisors. While his child was still alive there was hope, and he could *do* something. He prayed and fasted for whole nights just lying on the ground (verse 16). He prayed desperately to God for the child's healing. It did not happen. Now there is nothing left to pray for. It is out of David's hands entirely so he continues with his life. 'Life is for the living' appears to be David's mentality, and so, while not exactly joyful, he is able to move on and look to the future. While this sounds very unfeeling of David, and even his advisors are surprised, it does reflect the times in which he lived, where life was cheap, and infant mortality commonplace. So the verse, while a difficult one, does not support the idea that children are saved until they condemn themselves.

It is true that God on occasions did withhold punishment from children for the sake of the father in the Bible. Solomon benefited in this way in 1 Kings 11:34. However, the way that God spoke to Solomon in 1 Kings 11 had nothing to do with the innocence of a child. Solomon was king and a fully responsible adult when God spoke to him then. The passage had nothing to do with God preserving the innocence of a covenant child, but everything to do with the undeserving mercy of God on an adult. That doctrine is well covered in the Bible, but nothing to do with our discussions here.

*Summary* From the three passages considered, which are usually taken as biblical support of this position, we have seen that there is actually no biblical warrant to do so at all.

## (b) Individual responsibility

The chief difficulty of this position is that it takes away the notion of individual responsibility. If a child can be saved due to the actions of the parent, salvation is not entirely and only due to the individual's actions. This is not the teaching we see elsewhere though. Ezekiel 18:2–4 makes it clear that the child is not punished for the father's sins. Therefore it seems unreasonable that the opposite is true: that a child can be rewarded for his father's faith by salvation.

The idea that children of Christian parents will go to heaven until they personally choose disobedience is a nice comfortable thought, but there are difficulties. There is a lack of textual support, and the texts regularly quoted are clearly insufficient. The position seems to rest mainly on the idea of covenant. We will discuss this in a later chapter.

*(c) How long is the age of innocence?*

The thought that a child is covered by the faith of his parents until he can choose for himself is very comforting. There is no convincing textual proof that such a position is acceptable and we have a problem in applying it. If a child is covered by the faith of the parents until they choose for themselves, we need to define when a child is free to choose.

*(i) The biblical evidence*     The Old Testament does not explicitly discuss the issue, but there are indications that young children were not held morally responsible for their behaviour. Deuteronomy 1:39 mentions children who 'do not yet know good from bad'. Therefore they clearly are not being regarded as accountable, because they are too young. Similarly, Isaiah 7:15, when speaking of the Messiah, says that there will come a time in the child's life when he will be able to know right from wrong. There appears to be an age of innocence before that point, at least in terms of human behaviour. How long does this last for? We need to develop some workable guidelines for this.

*(ii) Israelite definitions*     Other definitions of the age of responsibility have been tried. Parents in the Old Testament grounded their children in the Torah, looking to the day when the child would have learned enough from God to bear the burden of responsibility himself. Later Judaism fixed a date for this, at thirteen, and marked it with a special ceremony, the Bar Mitzvah. More recent Judaism has also developed a ceremony for the girls at the age of twelve called the Bath Mitzvah.

Is this an age limit that we can use to suggest that now a child becomes accountable before God? It looks very unlikely,

because to do so is to change the regular purpose of the Bar
Mitzvah ceremony. It was originally meant as a human
'coming of age ceremony', rather as an eighteenth birthday
party in British society is. Both mark the 'coming of age'
rather than any specifically theological position about spiritual innocence. Therefore neither can give us guidelines in this
matter.

The Bible would not try in any place to defend the idea that
a child is innocent and is not accountable before God until
the age of thirteen. There are cases, as we have seen, where
God clearly has chosen and used children younger than this
as his servants, for example Samuel in 1 Samuel 3, or
Jeremiah in Jeremiah chapter 1.

From an experiential position it is also difficult to defend.
It is difficult to consider that God would declare innocent
(because of the faith of the parents) a twelve-year-old
monster, despite (potentially) rape, murder, theft, and any of
hundreds of other crimes that the twelve-year-olds of today
commit. This, however, is an emotive not a theological
response, and a judge might well instruct the jury to strike
this comment from the record!

The Bar Mitzvah also related to the age of consent. Our
society today has also changed the usual marriageable age
and age of consent. It is more usually eighteen or twenty
when people leave home or get married. Does this mean that
in our society they are still covered by the faith of the parents,
and therefore able to enter heaven until the age of eighteen (or
equivalent to the Bar Mitzvah)? This seems to be extremely
unreasonable.

There were probably other ages that were important for
young Israelites. One of these may relate more closely to our
modern eighteenth or twenty-first birthday, when within
Israel, as in our own society, the person has reached greater

maturity, and receives greater responsibility. This could be our sought after 'age of accountability'. Some commentators[17] suggest that Numbers 14:28–31 referring to Israelites under the age of twenty suggests that they were only junior members of society.

This is because God did not count any Israelites under the age of twenty as being involved or responsible for the lack of faith in God that resulted in them wandering in the desert for forty years. God seems to have counted anyone under twenty as innocent if we compare this with another passage that describes these same people in the same situation: 'And the little ones that you said would be taken captive, your children who do not yet know good from bad – they will enter the land' (Deuteronomy 1:39). This is reflected also in the 'head tax' of Exodus 30:14, where during a census of the population, only adults of over twenty had to give a money gift to God in thanks for their salvation.

It is also true that only men of twenty years and over were considered fit for military service (see Numbers 1:3 and 2 Chronicles 25:5), something that is not true of the Israeli military today. So does the Old Testament teach that the child remains a child, and therefore non-accountable to God, until they are twenty? This seems even more unreasonable than the previous figure of thirteen.

While these last two figures of thirteen and twenty certainly point to important stages in the development of the man or woman, they are surely not there to suggest that God does not know their sins and hold them guilty for them. They represented then, as they still do, important stages in the development of the person and their acceptance of responsi-

---

17 R. E. Clements, 'The Relation of Children to the People of God in the Old Testament', in *Baptist Quarterly*, 21:5 (January 1966), p. 198.

bility, but do not mean that the person has no responsibility before this point. Even in today's society we see this. Teenagers, while certainly protected under modern law, can still be found guilty of crimes, and personally punished for them, though we also have more direct and severe punishments for the over-eighteens, and speak more freely about their responsibility. These ages in ancient Israel appear to reflect the same sort of approach. They are not then indications that the child was innocent before God up to those ages.

*(iii) Psychological aspect*    From the perspective of current human psychological studies, this time of personal rebellion and responsibility could be defined as the time when children first say 'no'! This is the stage when they begin to resist the will of the parent, perhaps accompanied by a turning away of the head from the bottle, or spoonful of food. This happens at a very early age indeed. 'No' is usually one of the first words a child will learn. If this is the moment of active rebellion against the commandment 'honour thy father and mother', and therefore counts as a specific sin, then the debate of an age of innocence can only apply to very young infants and stillborn children. All other ages have already condemned themselves by saying 'no'. Certainly any child old enough to respond to the simplest sentence is, by that stage, a sinner in need of saving.

Perhaps, rather than looking at a specific stage in a child's development, we should be looking for developmental stages.[18] At what point decision-making passes from parents to children is something that cannot be fixed. It comes gradually and differs from one to another. 'Do it because I say so' hopefully gradually becomes 'do it because it is right'. This

18 Eric Lane, *Special Children?*, p. 55.

debate will be examined in more detail in a later chapter, but as we can see, actually defining such a moment is technically very difficult.

*(iv) Does a lack of moral awareness have to equal innocence?*[19]
Perhaps this whole supposition that a lack of moral awareness equals a state of innocence before God is incorrect. The fact that children of certain ages lack a sense of moral awareness does not necessarily mean that they can be regarded as being in a state of innocence. In fact the opposite appears to be the case, from both biblical and psychological perspectives. Children appear rather to be born in a state of blindness to right and wrong, often resulting in them defying moral behaviour rather than conforming to it. This is what we would expect from the traditional definition of original sin.

*Summary* The 'age of innocence' does not appear to be a biblical concept, nor does it seem clear as to when any such age (should it exist) might be. The Old Testament recognises simply that a child belongs under the influence of his family until a certain age. That family influence and authority does not mean that the child is innocent, or covered by the family's faith. It merely places before the child an opportunity of learning about God. The psalmist sheds further light on this issue when he says: 'Even from birth the wicked go astray' (Psalm 58:3). The psalmist is speaking of children who certainly would be considered under their parents' authority and responsibility, yet are described as 'astray' from a spiritual perspective. At least this is true of the children of the 'wicked'. From this then it would appear necessary to say that at least infants of unbelieving parents are unsaved,

---

19 *Ibid.*, p. 52.

though it may still be possible to say that children of believing parents may come under covenant benefits.

From these conclusions then, and making the most benevolent assumptions possible, there are severe limits under which a dying child may be said to go to heaven:

- If we assume that the covenant relationship of a parent makes a difference to the state of an infant; if the child is born of believing parents, then they come under this covenant agreement with God, and are saved. This assumption will be tested in a later section.
- Let us assume the most obviously workable definition of the 'age of innocence' as that of infanthood, before the child first learns to defy rules and say 'no'. Using this definition, we could defend a position that suggests that children below a certain age may be saved due to their innocence. This second position can only be held if the difficulties inherent in the doctrine of original sin can be dealt with satisfactorily.

Making these assumptions, the position remains unhelpful in the main, because there are not many children to which it applies. It could bring comfort in the tragic circumstances of a stillborn child, or a baby's death, but little more than that. More importantly, it has to make some rather large assumptions that have not been very well defended in the above discussion.

So, making the best possible assumptions, we could only offer the hope of heaven to:

1.  babies of unsaved parents from birth (or possibly conception) until the close of the 'age of innocence' (however long that is);

2. babies of saved parents (until they pass beyond parental authority at an undefined age).

After these conditions, all would be condemned to hell unless they had responded to Christ by faith.

## 3. Guilty until made innocent

'For as in Adam all die, so in Christ all will be made alive' (1 Corinthians 15:22). This position takes considerable notice of the doctrine of original sin. The usual teaching with regard to this doctrine, as we saw above, is that the person is guilty before God. Blame is laid at their door regardless of whether they ever committed a blameworthy act, and that they are guilty by their association with Adam initially. Humans are therefore by nature guilty before God. This idea[20] clearly relates to newly born children even though they have committed no blameworthy acts or experienced guilty feelings.

Following this idea of original sin through suggests that there is a time in a child's life when he is unable to comprehend, let alone respond to, the gospel; and yet the child remains under the judgement of God. This seems unfair and harsh. Yet putting the pragmatic approach aside, it does seem to be the theological teaching of Scripture: 'Folly is bound up in the heart of a child' (Proverbs 22:15); 'a child left to himself disgraces his mother' (Proverbs 29:15).

As children are under the influence of original sin, they are naturally part of the fallen human race. Therefore they come under the condemnation of Adam, as Paul wrote: 'For as in Adam all die, so in Christ all will be made alive' (1 Corinthians 15:22; see also Romans 5:12).

---

20 *Ibid.*, p. 49.

The position seems clear-cut and simple; there can be no false comforts given for the bereaved, whatever the age of their dead loved one. This view is uncomfortable and uncompromising, but it appears to be strong biblically.

Many theologians would say that maintaining that children are not born in Adam and thus are not subject from birth to condemnation and death is to deny the plain teaching of Scripture. Further, some would also say that having Christian parents couldn't move a child from union with Adam into union with Christ.

It is difficult to deny that this is scriptural, and it is totally in accord with the doctrine of original sin, yet it is a very hard doctrine to accept pastorally and theologically. It is hard enough to tell the parents of a stillborn child that God is a loving God, yet to tell them in the same breath that this child has gone to hell as a sinner is pastorally monstrous.

So what can we say? Here there seems to be a clear biblical position, which it would be comfortable to avoid for the sake of infants particularly. Is our desire to do this part of the fierce protective attitude that we feel towards children, or is there a logical theological reason?

*Summary*

This position insists on the importance of the doctrine of original sin. That, in itself, is sufficient to define the position of infants in relation to God. They are all sinners from conception because they are made from fallen human nature, and bear within them the curse of God, as does all of the fallen creation. There can be no escape from this except through personal individual salvation. There is only one way to be saved.

The strength of this argument is the biblical teaching on this point in relation to adults. The difficulty of this argument is that it seems so harsh and unlike the God we considered in Chapter 1 of this book.

## 4. We don't know and the Bible does not say

> Jesus did many other things as well. If every one of them were written down, I suppose that even the whole world would not have room for the books that would be written. (John 21:25)

The Bible does not actually make an issue out of this particular question. Some suggest in opposition to some of the above statements[21] that there is no biblical evidence that a gentile child below the 'age of innocence' can be saved. However, it would be equally true to say that there is no definitive evidence in Scripture that teaches that infant children will be lost either.[22] Perhaps a position of reverent and hopeful agnosticism is the best place to be. We dare not add to Scripture, but neither can we decide from Scripture that God cannot or will not save all children dying in infancy.

We are merely reaching for information the Bible does not give us. It is not really surprising that we lack biblical information on this matter. This doctrine of original sin is the theological teaching of Scripture towards consenting adults. Nowhere does Scripture actually apply this doctrine, or any other teaching, to unaware infants. Therefore we must also be cautious in doing so. The Bible teaches only about adults who are accountable.

Theologically we could also say that rigidly applying this doctrine in this context is a very harsh and hard-line approach, focusing on one aspect of the character of God,

---

21 L. Berkhof, *Systematic Theology* (Banner of Truth, 1939), p. 638.
22 Eric Lane, *Special Children?*, p. 61.

namely his anger at sin. To balance our picture of God, we also have to remember that God remains a God of mercy even if (as in the case of the parents of a stillborn child) we cannot understand all he gives. As always, we need to seek a balance, and all the facets of God's character must remain true about him at the same time. We need to find a way of holding the different views of God together in arriving at a balanced attitude to this problem.

As we cannot find a passage that tells us specifically of the fate of unborn children, we need to be careful and sensitive. We can apply other theological principles here as well as that of original sin. We can, for instance, consider that both unborn babies and the newly born have not heard the gospel in a way they can understand and respond to. Therefore they are not fitted for hell. God will not condemn someone who has had no chance to respond and choose the right way. Under this concept, God would judge babies in the same way that he would those who have never heard the gospel; that is, that they are judged according to the light they have received.

If the miracles that were performed in you had been performed in Tyre and Sidon, they would have repented in sackcloth and ashes. But I tell you, it will be more bearable for Tyre and Sidon on the day of judgement than for you. (Matthew 11:21–22)

We can also plead for mercy from God and quote Abraham in saying 'Will not the Judge of all the earth do right?' (Genesis 18:25).

Perhaps it is also possible to argue from the book of Jonah that God has a care for even the unsaved who have not heard, let alone for these infants who have not heard:

But Nineveh has more than a hundred and twenty thousand

people who cannot tell their right hand from their left, and many cattle as well. Should I not be concerned about that great city? (Jonah 4:11)

If God has a heart as big as this for unsaved people, then surely unsaved infants who could be described as innocent will be safe in God's care. This is a nice argument, but not a particularly accurate textual one.

This position therefore must focus on applying all the principles that arise from the other positions above. The three issues considered to have importance so far are:

1. original sin;
2. the justice of God;
3. judgement according to opportunity.

However, when considering these issues, we can see that they have all been applied out of the context in which they originally arose. Each of the three issues actually addresses other questions rather than this one. It is quite possible that its meaning has been stretched beyond that given in the original context by applying it to this different issue. Therefore each of these three points needs treating with caution in this context. We cannot take any one of them and dogmatically assert that this is the true biblical position on infant salvation. We need to include each of the issues in a picture of the nature of God.

Practically speaking, this means that we cannot consider a particular proof text, nor argue fiercely for one line or doctrine. We have to assert with the Bible that

- God is holy and cannot have anything to do with sin;
- God has judged the world, and original sin is part of that judgement;

- God is just and perfect, therefore any decision he makes will be perfect and just;
- it is God's will that all people everywhere come to repent (1 Timothy 2:3–4), and that God loves the helpless.

The bottom line is that we do not know, because the Bible does not say. Such a position is not very satisfying, but can be balanced by mentioning all the things that the Bible does say as in the paragraph above.

### Summary

This section then suggests that we cannot be dogmatic on the subject. Should we one day have to comfort a couple who have lost an infant, we might feel able to offer a hope, but could provide no certainties. Some principles would lead us one way, and other ideas another.

While this appears to be dodging the issue, it is no less than we can do with adults either. While all the life and testimony of any individual might make us certain that the adult is a believer, we always have to keep in the back of our minds Jesus' words:

'Not everyone who says to me, "Lord, Lord," will enter the kingdom of heaven, but only he who does the will of my Father who is in heaven. Many will say to me on that day, "Lord, Lord, did we not prophesy in your name, and in your name drive out demons and perform many miracles?" Then I will tell them plainly, "I never knew you. Away from me, you evildoers!"' (Matthew 7:21–23)

We cannot be certain that they really are believers, no matter how they behave. Conversely, any individual can personally be certain of salvation, because they alone with God really do know the true motives behind their confession of faith. The assurance of personal salvation is part of God's blessing to us through the Holy Spirit and biblical texts, for example John 1:12.

The actual salvation exercise is up to the sovereign God, and not a formula where if you do a, b and c, you will get salvation. Therefore we can never offer certain assurances of salvation on an individual basis, be they adult or child. What makes it particularly difficult is that the death of a baby is an extremely emotive subject. We would all like to be able to offer assurances of the child's salvation, but it is just not there in Scripture clearly enough. When counselling such a person, though, we do need to remember that God is

- a just God who will not be accused of injustice;
- a loving God who never willingly sends anyone to an eternity cut off from him.

## Conclusion

Having considered all the different views held generally within the church, the conclusion of the last section appears to be the most balanced, but the least satisfying. This is because it concludes that the Bible simply does not say. Nevertheless, there are several conclusions possible relating to the fate of the dying child:

1.  Children of unbelieving parents clearly come under the judgement of God from a very early age, because the ability to defy parents, and also God, is manifestly there within very young children.
2.  Children over the 'age of innocence' of believing parents are unsaved unless they personally have come to a faith in the saviour Jesus unless being a member of the covenant

is significant (see the next chapter).

3.  From conception up to the end of the 'age of innocence' (or parental accountability), the Bible simply does not address the question directly enough to be clear. We need to hold three different aspects of God in tension. Ultimately, with Abraham, we need to be confident in the justice and mercy of God. He will do what is right and just.

Perhaps in conclusion we could say along with some theologians[23] that if those who die in infancy are saved, it is not on the basis of their innocence but on the basis of the sovereign grace of God applied to them. How, or whether this is even possible, is a subject on which the Bible appears to be silent.

23 W. Hendrickson, *The Bible in the Life Hereafter*, (Baker, 1959), p. 103.

# 3

# *Covenant, Circumcision and Childhood*

One possibility we considered in the previous chapter was that if a child was circumcised, and accepted into the covenant community of Israel, then the child was saved by that means. This is important in our discussions.

The concept of a covenant is central to the Bible's teaching about God's love towards his people. But it is a complex issue, and the subject of a lot of theological research. Precisely what is meant by 'God's covenant', let alone 'entering into it', is not a simple matter for adults, let alone for an eight-day-old child.

## 1. What was the covenant?

'I am making my covenant of peace with him' (Numbers 25:12). Ever since the days of Noah and Abraham, the nation of Israel has been in a covenant relationship with God. Covenant simply means an agreement. From Genesis chapter 12 the story of what the covenant actually means unfolds through the pages of the Old Testament. A covenant at its most simple is merely a legal agreement between two parties.

Perhaps today we would use the term 'contract'. Dozens of secular covenant agreements have been discovered by archaeologists and translated, the majority of them made between 2000 and 1000 BC. The covenant God made with Abraham and Moses paralleled these very closely. The covenant God made with his people was an agreement in the same way that kings would make agreements with conquered nations. God has taken a known pattern and given it a new purpose.

Moving forward in time to the New Testament era, the usage of the word 'covenant' casts another interesting angle on the word's meaning. 'Covenant' in Greek (*diatheke*) can be equally well translated as 'testament'. Our 'New Testament' could be translated equally well as the 'new covenant'. The fact that there is a new one suggests a process of change over time. The 'old' one is no longer important, because a newer understanding and revelation has come. Some take this to mean that the old covenant is no longer needed, but this is a wrong understanding of the way God works: 'Do not think that I have come to abolish the Law or the Prophets; I have not come to abolish them but to fulfil them' (Matthew 5:17). God did not replace the old covenant with the new one, but rather he revised the covenant agreement regularly throughout the Old Testament, and did so again into the New Testament, updating it to the present circumstances, adding new information as he went. Through the centuries God has entered into a contract with humankind, which has been upgraded occasionally as his relationship with us was clarified. So to speak of a 'covenant' is to speak of a developing concept. Entering into God's covenant then has to be understood in the light of this process, which finished with the completion of the New Testament.

## (a) Noah's covenant

Noah received God's first covenant in Genesis 9:9–17. This was a promise not to flood the earth again. The rainbow was given as a sign of God's promise to remind people of his commitment to the human race. God's covenant with Noah did not need a human response. It was simply a promise from God for the world in general. It illustrates that the idea of covenant is a big one, not merely limited to Israel, nor to infants. We should not be too quick to simply equate the covenant with any one particular theological idea.

## (b) Abraham's covenant

The second covenant mentioned is with Abraham in Genesis 12:1–3. As with Noah, this involved promises given by God, rather than human obedience. God promised to give the land of Canaan to Abraham's descendants. He symbolised this covenant through an ancient ceremony also known from other cultures, in which sacrificial animals were split in two, and the parties making the covenant passed between the carcasses. Abraham didn't walk between the carcasses though; it was only certain symbols of God's presence that did so (Genesis 15:17). That suggested that the covenant was all of God's initiative. God was the only one who was tied to the covenant obligations at that time.

In an elaboration of the covenant with Abraham in Genesis 17, God gives another sign for the people in covenant relationship with God: that of circumcision. Abraham applies the sign to his household, and particularly his descendants, Ishmael and Isaac (Genesis 17:23–27). Abraham circumcised himself as a response to God's covenant with him (Genesis 17:24). All the subsequent members of the covenant people of Israel bore this sign to identify themselves. It was naturally costly, and permanent, for that was the nature of the covenant. Practised on Jewish boys of eight days old, it was a step taken by the parents of the child to demonstrate their obedience to God, and trust in him, and the child's involvement in the covenant people for the future. Circumcision was an act of obedience and love towards the covenant-making God. It was Abraham's response to God's overtures of love, and his family responded to God with him.

This practice of circumcision was not a new invention on God's part. Several Semitic and non-Semitic peoples also practised circumcision, according to extra-biblical sources.[1] On the other hand, other nations around at the time (for example the Philistines, see Judges 14:3) are described as uncircumcised. In modern times circumcision is still practised among Arabs and many African and Australasian tribes. The physical action itself therefore has to be considered insignificant, for many other societies also practise it, and it certainly does not bring membership into the covenant community. It is the symbolism that God has placed within it for Abraham that is more significant.

Being in this covenant meant two things for Israel in Abraham's time. First, God meant it to show that he had dedicated himself to Israel's care and protection. He was going to be their God, and would fulfil all the obligations of a God to them. That meant God would provide, bring fertility, make the sun shine and bring the rains, defeat the enemies, guide and lead in the right ways, show Israel all the good and perfect ways of living, and give them a land to live in. Second, it meant that Israel had to love and obey God. They had to

---

1 E. Stern, *Greek and Latin Authors on Jews and Judaism*, Vol.1 (The Israel Academy of Sciences and Humanities, 1984) pp. 2–4.

follow him alone, and not accept any other ideas about God, or any other ways of living. They would not follow any other ideas, for God would show them the best ways.

This covenant, as long as both parties stuck to it, guaranteed Israel's safety and their loving obedience to God. However, the rest of the Old Testament is the story of how Israel repeatedly broke it, and how God had to force them to return to the covenant with Abraham and his whole family, which includes his children. It was a corporate covenant.

God expected obedience as man's part in this covenant. It was never a gift given without strings for the receiver (though actually it often began that way, especially with Jacob). Once a person had responded to God, then God started to make demands on them, encouraging them to walk in his way. The whole of the life story of Jacob illustrates this beautifully.

The covenant was also clearly corporate, for the whole family was ratified as members of it individually and personally (look at Isaac in Genesis 26:2–3 and Jacob in Genesis 28:13–14). Their membership of the covenant community did not simply depend on the fact of their circumcision. It was not a corporate identification alone. As the people grew, circumcision needed to be added to with a personal calling from God. There were those who had been circumcised who passed out of the history of God's people, because they were not part of God's plans, and therefore could not be considered to be part of the covenant community, despite being circumcised. Ishmael and Esau were both circumcised as well as Isaac and Jacob, but it was only the last two who met with God personally and continued the promised line. The other two passed out of the nation of Israel, and its blessing.

*(c) Moses' covenant*

After the exodus, Moses brought his people God's rules at

Sinai for following the covenant that once more established them as God's people. Again it was set out in the ancient form of covenant between God and Israel. This time, though, the emphasis was all on what Israel needed to do for God. For twenty chapters of Exodus (chapters 20 to 40) this continues, either in rules or in the description of the Tabernacle and its function. The covenant with Moses focuses on the covenant responsibilities of Israel with God. There is no covenant sign here, unless it is the worship of God in the Tabernacle. The covenant here was made to acknowledge God's blessing and incredible commitment to their salvation (Exodus 19:4). But this time a response had to come from the people. The covenant was no longer unconditional. God described in detail what he wanted in the way of obedience. Covenant law was revealed to God's people, bringing responsibilities within the covenant relationship. The people accepted this responsibility in a solemn ceremony in which the covenant law was read from 'the book of the covenant' and 'the blood of the covenant' was sprinkled on the altar and on the people (Exodus 24:3–8). This ceremony was repeated in later generations. For instance, at the end of his life, Joshua calls the people together to rededicate themselves to God and to obey him (Joshua 24:15). They now have to obey God personally in order to remain in God's covenant, or they could be expelled from the nation. Leviticus 24:23 is an extreme example of this. The New Testament has the same idea when it speaks of 'putting out of fellowship'.

Moses does still follow the Abrahamic covenant as well. He is circumcised, and also circumcises his son, although he is a bit slow in doing this, for it does not happen until he is about eighty (Exodus 4:24–26), and his son is presumably an adult. The text does not say when Gershom, Moses' eldest son, was born, but it was certainly while he was still in Midian, and

Exodus 2:22 suggests that it was quite soon after the wedding to Zipporah. Clearly Moses did not consider circumcision at eight days old to be a particularly crucial part of the membership of the covenant. However, it was still a step of obedience that he had to take.

## (d) Beyond Moses

The concept of covenant continued through the Old Testament, with God revealing new aspects of it to David (with the importance of the line of David and the Messiah being a son of David, see 2 Samuel 7:8–16) and Jeremiah particularly (Jeremiah 31:31). The covenant relationship, however, did not change; there was merely more understanding of how God was going to be able to achieve his promises. The people were still part of the covenant people, and still enjoyed all the benefits of being in covenant membership, and still had to follow all the obligations of it as well. The issue of circumcision as a sign of the covenant also remained. Passover for instance was forbidden to those who had not been circumcised (see Exodus 12:48). The tie between entering into the Promised Land and circumcision as covenant obedience is another example of the need to be both obedient and circumcised as a Jew. This is reflected in the Israelites' circumcision at Gilgal after the entry into the Promised Land (Joshua 5:2–9). However, in the new teaching and discussion God brought through David, Jeremiah, Ezekiel and others, circumcision was clearly not the focal point of the covenant. God focused more on their obedience and lifestyle. It was a circumcision of the heart that God was particularly concerned with, not of the flesh (1 Samuel 15:22).

## Summary

Covenant is a developing concept, which began as kingly

treaties with conquered peoples that God developed to explain his promises for the salvation of his people, his blessings upon those people, and the obligations of those people to respond to the covenant laws, or be cut off. Circumcision was a symbol of physical membership within the family of this covenant. Later revelation of the covenant demonstrated that genuine membership was actually conditional on obedience to the laws, not on the symbol, which was in any case merely borrowed from secular experience. While circumcision gave you the right to join, and become part of the nation of God, it was always personal commitment issuing in obedience that ultimately mattered for an individual's salvation.

## 2. What was circumcision a sign of?

'It will be the sign of the covenant between me and you' (Genesis 17:11). If then circumcision was not the main part of the covenant fulfilment, what role did it play? Why bother with it at all?

Circumcision was a sign of the covenant made to Abraham, and was to be used specifically with eight-day-old boys from that point on. It identified those who were subjected to the conditions of covenant obedience by their parents. It clearly then relates to the issue we discussed in the previous chapter. What is the state of babies who die while within the covenant of God? Can we suggest that the circumcised child is saved and going to heaven from that point onwards? If the child dies in early infancy, then will it be safe from hell?

If the answer to these questions is yes, then the answer to the difficulties in the previous chapter becomes a lot easier.

## (a) Circumcised and saved

If circumcision was a sign of membership into God's covenant, and therefore signified the spiritual safety of that child, then the problem is solved, and merely needs to be applied to a New Testament and modern scenario. Some paedobaptists feel that it is right to link modern infant baptism to circumcision.[2] This means that the child born into a believing home has the right to the mark of belonging, even when he is too young to fulfil the conditions on which the covenant was made. As Israelite babies were accepted into Israel on the day of circumcision, even though they were totally unaware of the event's significance, so infants today are brought into the covenant community of the church through baptism. This event will be later ratified or repudiated by the youngster as they either choose to be confirmed, or reject the offer. At this point, they are making their own choices, and are responsible. Before that, they are covered by their parents' faith.

However, the problem is more complex than this simple equation: circumcision = covenant membership = saved and going to heaven. This equation is also not true to the way the Old Testament uses the idea of covenant membership, which we examined previously. Paedobaptists do not usually make such a blunt and simplistic statement either.

The major difference between this equation and the Old Testament view of circumcision appears to be that adult covenant obedience was clearly far more important for salvation than circumcision. This leads to a more subtle understanding of the purpose of circumcision and infant

---

2   Michael Green, *Baptism, Its Purpose, Practice and Power* (Hodder & Stoughton, 1987), p. 66.

baptism. Paedobaptists would argue that this rite merely gave the infant the right to follow the teaching and receive the opportunity to be blessed by God. Infant baptism, when viewed in this way, does not affect our standing before God 'until and unless we cash the cheque',[3] and claim personally what has been made over to us by God. So you are not 'saved' if you remain a baptised unbeliever, but you bear the mark of how much God cares for you. Circumcision then, in the paedobaptist position, suggests a pointer, a hope by the parents, which does not save, but gives the child help in that it points the way to God for them in ways that the uncircumcised may not discover.

Modern Jewish thinking is different. Modern Jews[4] appear to think that circumcision is a beautifying act, an attempt to perfect the creation begun by God; and indeed an act of sacrifice: a giving up of a part for the sake of the whole. The act makes them more beautiful and therefore acceptable to God. It is not for salvation, but a mark of obedience, wanting to be beautiful for God.

Biblical Judaism also did not see circumcision as something bringing salvation, but rather an act of obedience to God, and dedication to him. Israelites were commanded to circumcise not only their children but also their servants, both native and foreign (Genesis 17:12–13).[5] Only circumcised foreigners who were servants or resident aliens could share in the Passover, the feast of the Israelite community (Exodus 12:43). To be uncircumcised was to be outside the covenant. It was therefore more like a membership card than anything else.

---

3   *Ibid.*, p. 90.
4   A. Wood, *Judaism* (Batsford Academic and Educational Press, 1984), p. 10.
5   Gill Dallow, *Children's Ministry* magazine, Issue 7, p. 6.

The standard interpretation of circumcision even among the Jews of Jesus' day had little to do with the covenant.[6] Circumcision was a sign of being within the election of Israel and the children of Abraham. It was a mark of being Jewish rather than of anything else.

The famous Jewish philosopher Philo lived in Alexandria at about the time of Jesus. Among other things, he tried to reinterpret Judaism in terms of Greek philosophy. As such, Philo often forms a bridge between ancient Jewish thinking patterns and a modern Western world-view which is based on this Greek philosophical world-view even today. He saw circumcision not as a rite 'whereby a male child gains entry into the congregation of Israel', but rather a sign of the faith or lack of it in the parents. In other words, it was a rite for parents rather than children. If this is the case, and if Philo was right in his understanding of circumcision, then we need to be thinking of it and its relation to the salvation of an infant in a very different way.

There are therefore some things that we can clearly say about the significance of circumcision:

*(i) It is not for salvation*[7]    It is often assumed that a child within the covenant relationship is saved because of that covenant, and that this stays the same until the child by their own free choice rejects the covenant of God by their behaviour. For a child of the covenant, a call to personal decision

---

6  E. P. Sanders, *Judaism Practice and Belief,* p. 213.

7  For the purpose of clarity, the terms 'salvation' and 'saved' refer to the state in which an Israelite is forgiven, enjoying a personal relationship with God, and ultimately will be going to heaven. We will use the terms 'in covenant membership' and 'covenant people' to refer to Israelites who are certainly part of Israel, and in receipt of the general blessings of God on that nation, but are not necessarily personally saved themselves.

would mean deciding not to follow God, because they were born into a state of following him. While this sounds encouraging for the child, it is only a common assumption and does not actually reflect the reality of the biblical teaching on covenant membership.

Children are certainly not saved by the physical act of being circumcised. This has already been seen above in the cases of Ishmael and Esau, but it is also clearly demonstrated by considering the female children, who were not circumcised. Though the ancient communities had little place for women in public, nobody tries to suggest that females were not saved. If circumcision alone was the qualification for salvation, then all the females of the population would be lost. Going back to the time of Abraham, his wife Sarah was clearly part of God's plans, and saved, even though uncircumcised. God came to deal specifically with her (see Genesis 18:12–14), and renew the Abrahamic covenant promise to her through a rather comical exchange. Rahab is another example of a woman who was clearly saved, physically as well as spiritually (Joshua 2:9–14). We can speak about her spiritual salvation because she is mentioned among the honoured and chosen people in the genealogies of the line of the Messiah Jesus in Matthew 1:5. So, the fact that females were clearly in a saved relationship with Yahweh without being circumcised suggests that the physical act of circumcision alone was not crucial for salvation.

*(ii) You can be circumcised but not saved*  There were also people who were part of God's covenant community physically, born of Jewish parents, who bore the mark of circumcision, but because of their refusal to accept God's power and might personally for themselves, remained outside of God's salvation. Though they were physically part of the

covenant people, their behaviour placed them outside of it. Eli's sons are an example of this. As the sons of the high priest, we can assume that they were circumcised, and considered themselves to be part of the covenant community. More than that, they were actively serving priests themselves (1 Samuel 1:3) and so their circumcision can be taken for granted. However, their spiritual standing can't. The two sons were ungodly, and came under God's judgement for it (1 Samuel 3:14). We can say then that circumcision began the child's teaching about God, for this confirmed that they were part of the covenant people, with those privileges of access to knowledge. It meant no more than this and said nothing about the spiritual state of the child, actual or potential.[8] Not all circumcised people were spiritually alive. Ishmael was circumcised, but he was denied the blessings of the covenant given to Isaac (Genesis 17:20).

*(iii) You can be saved but uncircumcised*   There were also Jews within the covenant community who had not been circumcised. Joshua 5:1–3 speaks of 'the children of Israel' who are clearly considered as part of the covenant community, but goes on to mention that they were uncircumcised. This is because all the children born since the exodus had not been circumcised, and all those (except Joshua and Caleb) who left Egypt in the exodus, and were circumcised, had since died. So we have a whole nation of covenant people who are identified as Jews and who clearly believe and are saved. They accept that God has just brought them into the Promised Land (Joshua chapter 4), though they are uncircumcised at the moment.

---

8   Eric Lane, *Special Children?*, p. 17.

*(iv) You can be non-covenant, uncircumcised, but saved anyway*
Conversely, there were also people who were not Jewish, and
had not been circumcised (though they usually became
circumcised later on), whom God treated as members of the
covenant community and blessed. They were known as God-
fearers. The Jews clearly considered them to be saved, and
worshippers of God, but as yet outside the covenant community and its privileges. They would remain so until becoming
full proselytes. They had a specific process by which this
could happen. This involved fulfilling the Jewish demands of
circumcision (males), which related one to the covenant (see
Galatians 5:3), baptism (males and females), which made one
ritually clean, and an offering (males and females) in the
Jerusalem Temple, which atoned for sin.

## *(b) Membership of Israel*

So circumcision gave entry into one level of God's people, but
not into the level which guaranteed salvation. It is possible
then to speak of Israel in two ways: the nation, which was
circumcised and nominally at least obeying God's laws; and
then on a different level the saved and chosen people of God.
This distinction is seen in the church as well. We can speak of
the church visible, that is people in churches who at least
claim to be Christians, though we know by their lives and by
bitter experience that some will not be. We can also speak of
the church universal, which is the true collection of Christians
throughout the world. The church we see has to be the first of
those, as the Jewish nation also had to be. Only God knows
whether a person is really saved or not. It was true in the old
covenant with Ishmael and Esau. It was also true in the new,
with Simon Magus and possibly Ananias and Sapphira. In
the fallen world there is no possibility of having a completely
'pure' church. Not only is every member flawed and defiled,

but also there is no certain way of discerning the 'hypocrite' from the 'genuine'. We can only hear a person's profession, look at his life, and make a provisional assessment; it is God alone who can see into the heart.[9]

So membership of the covenant through circumcision (or its New Testament parallels) gives people opportunities to hear God and become part of the visible church, but does not actually save them. The church is (as was the Jewish nation) full of people who have this privileged access, but who are not saved.

Circumcision then was a witness to God's general work of salvation, not to the faith growing in the heart of an individual. It was an external sign required for membership in the external community of God, through which access to God was possible.[10]

This shows that while circumcision was required for full membership into the covenant nation of Israel, it was not needed for entering into relationship with God for salvation. For that, merely becoming a God-fearer was sufficient. What mattered most was not the outward sign, but inward devotion and obedience to God, which was found in a God-fearer as well as in a fully orthodox, circumcised Jew. Ezekiel summarises this well by focusing on the importance of the heart in saying:

> This is what the Sovereign LORD says: No foreigner uncircumcised in heart and flesh is to enter my sanctuary, not even the foreigners who live among the Israelites. (Ezekiel 44:9)

---

9   Michael Green, *Baptism, Its Purpose, Practice and Power*, p. 84; see also 1 Samuel 16:7: 'Man looks at the outward appearance, but the LORD looks at the heart.'

10  *Ibid.*, p. 76.

*(c) Of the heart*

When talking about circumcision, the Old Testament refers to the circumcision of the heart in particular. Of the two circumcisions, heart and flesh, this was the most important:

> The LORD your God will circumcise your hearts and the hearts of your descendants, so that you may love him with all your heart and with all your soul, and live. (Deuteronomy 30:6)

> Circumcise yourselves to the LORD, circumcise your hearts,
> you men of Judah and people of Jerusalem,
> or my wrath will break out and burn like fire
> because of the evil you have done. (Jeremiah 4:4)

So, while circumcision is an outward symbol of obedience made to the covenant God, it is no more than that. Real covenant obedience, real circumcision, is a matter for the heart. This meant that God could not accept people who were physically part of the covenant community who were in reality outside of the blessings of God because they had broken the covenant laws.

So to be a full member of God's covenant community in the Old Testament in good standing with God (and therefore 'saved'), you had to be willing to obey God in whatever he commanded. This included physical circumcision for males, but also you had to be prepared to try and live your life according to his ways (hence circumcised in heart). People who were circumcised in fact but not in heart (i.e. they lived in a way opposed to God) were not part of the covenant blessing. Solomon after completing the Temple was given a very serious warning about keeping his life right with God (1 Kings 9:6–7). True religion for God was circumcision of the heart, a life given over to God and his ways. It was a life of internal behaviour and faith. External factors were not as important as internal trust and obedience (see, for example, 1 Samuel 15:22 or Isaiah 1:14).

All this is very different from physical circumcision, where the only qualification was to have Israelite parents willing to perform the act.[11] There is no idea of faith, repentance, obedience, trust or any other quality being necessary in order to be physically circumcised.

*Summary*

Circumcision, while being a significant and important part of the covenant obligations, was not vital to salvation, and did not have transforming power in and of itself. Any Jew wanting to be serious about God and have a relationship with him had to be circumcised, in the same way that they had to obey the Ten Commandments. It was a matter of obedience rather than salvation. When we speak of circumcision, then, it is the circumcision of the heart rather than the flesh that God considers most significant. It was the inward attitude that led to the outward action. This is nothing strange, but finds expression in the New Testament too, especially in the book of James with his emphasis on faith being worked out in actions (James 2:17).

This all lessens the significance of an eight-day-old's actual circumcision. What matters more is what as a child, boy and adult he does with this opportunity.

## 3. What of the infant?

'For the generations to come every male among you who is eight days old must be circumcised' (Genesis 17:12). What

---

11 Eric Lane, *Special Children?*, p. 14.

does all this mean for the salvation of an eight-day-old? The Old Testament commands that a boy of eight days old be circumcised. Obviously a child as young as that is not capable of responding to God from the heart in obedience in the same way that Abraham did and that God values most. So circumcision must have an alternative significance which is relevant to an eight-day-old baby. Circumcision relates to becoming a child of the covenant. Yet, precisely what that means still has to be clarified. It certainly means the following things for an eight-day-old:

- To have a place in the community, and come under the protection of God, even from eight days old.
- To be free to worship God and join in all the times of celebration.
- To know God is willing to forgive your sins, and following your parents to obey God's commands.
- To look forward to entering into the covenant relationship as an adult in a wider sense, at the Bar Mitzvah, when the boy child becomes an adult. There the child takes on the wider responsibilities of worship and obedience, as befits an adult.
- To then be eligible for all the benefits of being one of the people of God, with a land, hope and future all promised to you, and the great God being your personal God.

This works well as a definition of covenant membership, but the five points don't speak about any salvational benefits for an eight-day-old. What salvational state is the eight-day-old boy actually in? He certainly has no knowledge or control over what is going on, and he equally certainly has not personally chosen to obey God and live by his principles. What then can outward circumcision mean for him and his state before God? There seems to be three possibilities here.

(i)   He is a 'child of God' in a covenant relationship with
      God personally because of his circumcision alone. He is
      considered as belonging to God, and subject to the
      corporate salvation of his family and nation.
(ii)  He is a 'child of God', forgiven and saved, because of his
      family's trust in God – by proxy, as it were.
(iii) He is merely an Israelite with physical benefits of
      belonging to a closed community, but the actual fact of
      his circumcision as a child has nothing to do with his
      salvation. He is not actually a 'child of God' at all at the
      moment, merely being privileged at having parents who
      will bring him up in the 'nurture and admonition of the
      Lord'.

*(a) Following up possibility (i)*

We have concluded that circumcision is merely a sign. The
significance of the sign is not its salvational powers, but its
reminder of the potential of God's salvation. Nobody, least of
all an eight-day-old child who cannot understand symbolism,
can be saved by an outward symbolic observance. This possibility then appears to be outside of the usual concept of
circumcision within the Old Testament.

*(b) Following up possibility (ii)*

Israelite faith is corporate faith. The nation worships God
together, obeys God together, or suffers under God's hand
together. The nation is saved together, and families certainly
are saved together. This possibility suggests that the child
belongs to God because of the faith that the parents have in
God. There is certainly a strong argument and good biblical
evidence for this. Families are considered to be of the same

faith as the family head. Whole families were to convert at the same time. Rahab's whole family was saved (literally and presumably also spiritually) at the fall of Jericho due to Rahab's faith (Joshua 2:18). In the New Testament we see the case of the Philippian jailer (Acts 16:33). This possibility will be examined further below.

### (c) Following up possibility (iii)

Circumcision at this stage is an expression of the parents' faith, not the child's. It is an expression of the family's trust in God, and that they are committing their child into the care of God and his covenant community. The parents are saying to God, 'Look, here is another child. We intend to be, and indeed are being, obedient in fulfilling your commands in relation to this infant.' What appears to be happening is that the parents (particularly the father, who is the head of the household) are expressing their faith in God, and their determination to raise the boy in full awareness of Yahweh and in obedience to all Yahweh's ways. The circumcision is an expressed desire of the parents that the child shall grow into a personal faith of his own, through his natural absorption of his parents' faith lived out daily, then personally expressed at his coming to manhood at his Bar Mitzvah. This appears to be most clearly in line with particularly the New Testament view on individual responsibility, which also appears in the Old Testament (see Jeremiah 31:29).

### Summary

Two possibilities remain. First, it is possible that the child has special status before God as a covenant child, and is saved until such time as the child finally chooses for himself. Alternatively, circumcision is a symbolic act, and the child is not saved, for the act only reflects the faith and commitment of the parents until such time as the child is able to choose or reject that faith for himself. The church generally is divided upon these two, and scriptural testimony is also ambiguous, so no conclusive solution that will be acceptable to all readers is possible here. The crucial issue however is that of the corporate nature of Israel's faith. Does this lead to real salvation or not?

## 4. Was it a corporate covenant?

'Do not hold against us the sins of the fathers' (Psalm 79:8). In order to apply this properly to our study, we still have to address this understanding of circumcision of the eight-day-old, and determine where they fit into Israel's covenant relationship with God. To understand the nature of the covenant more fully, we need to understand the nature of Israelite society, and so we have to go back to Scripture and the notion of family solidarity. Jewish and other ancient societies held that the faith of the father (usually the head of the household in biblical times) counted as the faith for the family as a whole.[12] Like an umbrella it 'covered' them all. God counted them all as members of the covenant relationship established through the father's faith. Individual members had no choice but to hold the same belief as the family head.

This headship idea can be carried further.[13] As Abraham was offered and accepted the covenant as the family head for all Israel, so all Israel was offered the covenant, and was accepted into the covenant by God even at the time of

---

12 Francis Bridger, *Children Finding Faith* (Scripture Union, 1988),
      pp. 132–3, see also John Inchley, p. 13.
13 *Ibid.*, p. 133.

Abraham. Moreover, this was not confined to adults who had made an open profession of faith in our modern sense. It applied to all Israelites, including children. This was emphasised in the rite of circumcision, which was not simply a ritual, but a sign established and commanded by God to show inclusion within the covenant.

Covenant theology here would suggest that Israel corporately has entered into a relationship with the living God. This is due first to Abraham's acceptance of God's covenant, and secondly to the acceptance of each subsequent family head. Faith in the Old Testament covenant style then appears to be a corporate thing, not an individual one:

> For the generations to come every male among you who is eight days old must be circumcised, including those born in your household or bought with money from a foreigner – those who are not your offspring. (Genesis 17:12)

Even those who are not blood relatives but part of the household are to be circumcised as a sign of inclusion in the covenant. In a home where there is at least one believing parent, it is their faith which appears to count for the rest of the household, until any one individual deliberately rejects God personally.

This suggests that children were to be treated as would-be believers, and saved, rather than as unbelievers. They were covenant children, they enjoyed all the rights and privileges of covenant relationship. They were welcome at all the ceremonies and festivals. They took part in much of what the nation was doing in worship, and God focused on their needs in particular ways. They were not outsiders but insiders, at least until they chose to exclude themselves from God's blessing.

## Summary

This then is the apparent meaning of the Old Testament covenant pattern. Some writers[14] consider this pattern has been carried across into the New Testament with the conversion of the Philippian jailer and of Crispus. However, even those writers[15] have to accept that children of the covenant eventually will have to be encouraged to appropriate the blessing they already possess as covenant children. The covenant alone does not save them.

We return to the conclusion mentioned above, that the Old Testament rite of circumcision allows the child to receive many benefits simply because their parent is a believer. But none of this has to do with salvation so much as being in a place where they can receive the teaching, protection and blessing which will help them to understand and know God. The corporate nature of Old Testament covenant then has to do with opportunities rather than actual salvation.

We can now attempt a definition of what the membership of the covenant community actually means for an infant. This can be made in two statements:

- The covenant community is best defined as the nation of Israel, among whom there are also unbelievers, rather as the church is today.
- Membership of this community merely places children within a position of privilege, where they can learn first-hand about God from experiencing him at work in their community, whereas other children born outside of God's covenant community have fewer and lesser opportunities to learn of God.

---

14 Francis Bridger, *Children Finding Faith*, p. 134.
15 *Ibid*.

This is presumably what Paul had in mind in his discussion in Romans 3:1–2:

> What advantage, then, is there in being a Jew, or what value is there in circumcision? Much in every way! First of all, they have been entrusted with the very words of God.

### 5. Moving forward into the New Testament

'Jesus has become the guarantee of a better covenant' (Hebrews 7:22). It is generally thought that the Old Testament covenant people were people who were saved on the basis of the covenant God made with them, through the sacrificial system. However, there appears to be a desire in the minds of many modern baptistic writers to remove any implications that this old covenant relationship can remain in force in the same way in the New Testament, or the present era, as it did in the Old Testament. There are often thought to be[16] three ways in which the old and new systems differ.

*(a) Covenant community*

While in the Old Testament God concentrated on making the children of his people into covenant children, to the exclusion of all others, in the New Testament, he frequently also reaches others.[17] This is certainly true in both New Testament studies and in our own experience. Children of Gentiles and unbelievers become Christians regularly. However, this does not mean that the system of covenant people has no place in the modern church, because God is doing a new thing among

---

16 For example Eric Lane, *Special Children?*
17 *Ibid.*, p. 31.

the Gentiles. There is still a benefit to be received from the access to the knowledge of God that being in the covenant community brings.

It was also never true that circumcision was God's only avenue of salvation in the Old Testament, and we have argued that actually it never was an avenue of salvation at all. There is no change in the application of God's salvation from the Old to the New Testament. It is all by faith, not any outward sign or ritual. God's offer of salvation always did apply to Gentiles as well as believers, the only significant difference being the number of Gentiles privileged to hear the good news in the New Testament period and beyond.

## (b) Salvation by ritual

Many people see the Old Testament method of salvation through the sacrificial system as being an outward empty observance that is irrelevant today. The sacrificial system remained part of the Law, which was to be replaced by grace. In the New Testament, covenant blessing is by faith alone. It is not dependent on ancestry, any ritual act, or even the rituals of baptism or the Lord's supper. Regeneration is the essence of the mode of entering the new covenant.[18]

Holding this option shows a wrong understanding of the purpose of the Old Testament covenant as we have seen it. The Old Testament faith always worked through external signs: Abraham's circumcision, the people's obedience to the Law, the sacrificial system, the Tabernacle worship etc., but that was never what saved them. Abraham was saved by faith (Romans 4:9), not by being a member of the covenant community of God. All the circumcision, sacrificial system and altar building Abraham undertook was of no use in

18 *Ibid.*, p. 32.

terms of salvation. It is true that God was pleased with his obedience, but the Bible continually insists that it was his faith which saved him and which issued in obedience: 'So those who have faith are blessed along with Abraham, the man of faith' (Galatians 3:9).

### (c) Salvation by parental teaching?

It is believed by some[19] that the two covenants, old and new, operated in another different way that has not yet been mentioned. The old covenant brought children to God by parental instruction and discipline. The new brings them to him by regeneration, which is not in the hands of the parents. This suggests that the Old Testament way of salvation is through parental instruction.

It is certainly true that parents in the Old Testament had a responsibility before God to raise their children in the 'training and instruction of the Lord'. However, that verse actually comes from Ephesians 6:4, and relates to the responsibility of fathers in the New Testament world as well. It is not fair to say that the children under the old covenant were saved by the discipline and teaching of their parents any more than it is to say that the children of the New Testament are. What saved both sets of children was the way in which the teaching and discipline of their parents and their community demonstrated what faith in God actually was, and encouraged them to accept faith for themselves. It was the outworking of the benefits of being in the covenant community. There was no difference in the method of salvation for old and new covenant children, any more than there was for adults.

---

19 *Ibid.*, p. 78.

*Conclusions*

1. For all children, as well as adults, salvation comes by the single route God has revealed to us: we all have to be saved individually through faith in the work of Christ and the regeneration of the Holy Spirit. This is such a fundamental teaching of the Bible that any interpretation of covenant or circumcision which challenges this has to be considered wrong. Under the old covenant this method of salvation was not fully revealed, but the fact that God would provide a way was somehow symbolised in all they did. It was their fundamental basis of belief, as it was their founding father Abraham's. God has not changed and neither has his method of salvation for a person of any age, in any time period.

2. A believer's children are not saved by virtue of being a believer's child. The concept of corporate salvation, family by family, or nation by nation, is attractive, but not in tune with the rest of the Bible if we separate the idea of salvation from the idea of Israel as a covenant nation, which we have found necessary.

We appear to have come to the following very negative conclusions about the state of being a covenant child:

(i) Children come into the world without a relationship with God.

(ii) They cannot be saved or regenerated through the faith of their parents.

(iii) Baptism, circumcision or any other ritual at any age cannot regenerate them.

*In what way are children of the covenant special?*

(i) They are special in that God has already given them to the parents as an answer to prayer, or as a special blessing. (See Sarah's reaction in Genesis 21:7, or Hannah's in 1 Samuel 1:20.)

(ii) They are set apart by God for a special opportunity to respond to him. They hear the word of God regularly at home, both directly and as a result of the lifestyle of the family and regular church attendance.

(iii) They pray and are prayed for by parents and others.

(iv) They have first-hand experience of God's involvement in their lives, by the example of the parents and a sense of God in the home.

In short, being a covenant child in the Old and New Testaments appears to mean that the child is unsaved, and remains unsaved initially, but with certain specific advantages over other children in relation to their opportunities to learn about God. This also applies to the children of believers today. They are not believers themselves until they make a personal commitment, but should, through the way their believing parents choose to live and exercise their parentage, have many opportunities and fewer barriers to come to faith than their contemporaries do. Believers' children have access to the means of regeneration which their parents have in their hands, whereas others must have an outside witness to it, which may not be as influential.[20]

## 6. Applying this to the conclusions of the previous chapter

We concluded in the last chapter that one reason for suggesting that an infant could be saved was on the basis of their membership of the covenant community. This section appears to dispel that possibility. Being a member of that

---

20 *Ibid.*, p. 81.

community through circumcision alone did not guarantee anything in terms of salvation upon the individual. It pointed to an opportunity for the child, but nothing more.

In the New Testament, or modern communities, a child raised in a Christian home, who is being taught the ways of God by example and practice, can also be said to be in the covenant community. They are in a position of opportunity and privilege that their contemporaries raised in secular homes do not have. It does not mean that they are saved, just that they have a clear opportunity to be saved, as they will have

- received a clear presentation of the gospel;
- good teaching and the example of parents and friends around them;
- people praying for them.

All this was true of a child in the time of Abraham, or David, or Jesus, and can be equally true today of a child in the home of a practising Christian. Whether the child is saved or not is ultimately up to God. Nothing has changed from the Old Testament to the New. What this means for the responsibilities of the parent and the church will be considered in the following chapters.

# Part Two
# THE FAMILY IN THE BIBLE

# 4

## *The Family in Old Testament Times*

The main influence upon most children's lives is the family,
and this has never been truer than in Old Testament times.
These days there are dozens of influences that impact upon
our children, such as television, computer games, fashion,
music and multicultural society to mention but a few. This
generation has many influences that shape its behaviour and
morals, some good, some not so good, and some distinctly
damaging. It is hardly surprising then that our generation is
growing up with such a wide diversity of interests, attitudes
and morals.

In ancient Israel, however, the family was the main place
where children gathered their role models in education and
life skills. Their parents, uncles and aunts, older brothers and
sisters and cousins were their heroes and mentors. There was
no cult television hero or sports person to play the role of,
nor a computer based adventure to live out.

God set out a pattern for the family to follow in giving the
children these role models. Practically speaking, all sorts of
different approaches were tried in Israel, both in the biblical
texts and presumably also in daily life. Israelite parents were

no more perfect than we are, and made many mistakes as we do. Those, while interesting, are not our focus, because we need a standard, an absolute, and a perfect rule to live by. We have made too many mistakes trying by experimentation to find the right ways to raise our children in this past generation. The next one deserves better. God's rules do give us this approach, if we will listen.

Today, parents are bombarded by advice about child-rearing from every conceivable angle. This is often contradictory and confusing. For the infant, 'Do I leave her to cry, or should I attend her?', for the toddler, 'Do I smack him when he breaks the rules, or will that emotionally scar him for life?' and so on, right into the terrible teenage years. For every expert opinion, there is another expert with the opposite one. In today's world there are no absolutes, and both parent and child are bombarded by contradictory input about growing up. By contrast, the only parental guide around for the Jews to follow was the Scriptures. In them, God had given the Jews a pattern to follow. That pattern was based on the wisdom of God for their society, and in a world of no absolutes, this formed a solid and reliable base from which to build. It is such a base that we need today.

## 1. Family relationships

'Children's children are a crown to the aged, and parents are the pride of their children' (Proverbs 17:6). In the Jewish family, children's respect for their parents would develop out of a good relationship with both God and their parents. Conversely, having a good relationship with God ideally required a good relationship with parents as well. This is because children were taught to 'honour their father and mother' in the Ten Commandments given in Exodus 20 and

Deuteronomy 5. There was an important link between the child's family and religious life. God was meant to be as central to their lives as their family was. So children were encouraged to keep close to both God and their parents.

The happiness of parents and children was bound up with one another, and reverence to God was the starting point for everyone. In this relationship, parents had many responsibilities to their children. The child was to be cared for, loved and provided for in Israelite society, in accordance with God's laws. This is very different from some of the other societies around at the time that followed other standards, where children were considered a necessary evil, or a possession to sell or dispose of as they wished, or a nuisance apprentice to be beaten into submission. The standard expected from children and parents was quite different.[1] In Israel, children were honoured and treasured (Proverbs 17:6) but nonetheless expected to obey their parents and pay attention to their teaching and advice (Exodus 20:12). That obedience had to come in many areas. This Old Testament code that describes how parents and children should relate to each other was quite radical for its time, and actually still is, if we are prepared to look at it closely. Applying it to our own situations and families may mean readjusting our thinking.

As a final comment in this area, God expects there to be a good relationship between child and parent. Even this most basic point is missed by so many. There is a breakdown of many family relationships in our society. Family relationships have to be worked on, but they are more often abandoned as dysfunctional.

So the first area to consider is that of relationships between parent and child, across which other relationships can be learned, such as the relationship between parent and God.

---

1  I. Smale, *A History of Children*, Vol.1 (Silverfish, 1998).

## 2. Discipline

'He who spares the rod hates his son, but he who loves him is careful to discipline him' (Proverbs 13:24). Parents who really loved their children were expected to discipline and correct them, especially when they were young. The phrase 'spare the rod and spoil the child' is quite well known, if sometimes abused by over-zealous parents. Nevertheless, it does represent biblical teaching (Proverbs 19:18 and Proverbs 23:13–14, for example), if not actually a biblical phrase itself. It is a subject well covered in other books, and will receive only a cursory inspection here.

As the Old Testament parents read their Scriptures, they learned that God expected a system of family discipline and correction that was based on his character and relationship with them. As parents, there are real and necessary boundaries that we must lay down, and God expects us to follow them. He has a real care for justice and fairness, and expects parents to exercise justice in their turn when operating these boundaries for the child's growth and development. The parents then have a responsibility before God to exercise fair discipline in the way that God would exercise it. As Israel's kings were expected to rule the nation as God wanted, so Israel's parents were expected to do the same with their children.

Parents have to make these boundaries clear and consistent. Not knowing where they stand really confuses children and causes them to become sneaky. They quickly learn how, when, and whom to ask for things. Adults who are watching the TV become good targets for 'Can I have a biscuit?', because they are not really listening to the importance of the request. However, if parents are available, and aware of you, they are probably not good targets, because they are then more aware of the fact that you had a biscuit only ten minutes ago. Children are wise to these things, so parents have to be alert and consistent.

Fairness and even-handedness is very important, and arises out of the justice God shows, and expects us to show also. Children also expect this. The phrase 'That's not fair' is very quick to come from a child's lips, even sometimes when it is perfectly fair. The principle has always been the same, merely brought down a few levels in society. A rule was a rule, applicable always, and to each member of the family equally, with an equal punishment meted out to all, on each occasion. If the children see the parents accepting God's authority, and living under it consistently and fairly, then they in turn are likely not only to accept God's authority, but their parents' authority too.

Coming to the more usually recognised issue of discipline, physical punishment, we find that God considered it a normal and necessary part of life's patterns. However, in the case of Israel, prescribed punishment was considerably less excessive than in the other societies around. There were commands in God's law to limit the extent of punishments:

> But if there is serious injury, you are to take life for life, eye for eye, tooth for tooth, hand for hand, foot for foot, burn for burn, wound for wound, bruise for bruise. If a man hits a manservant or maidservant in the eye and destroys it, he must let the servant go free to compensate for the eye. And if he knocks out the tooth of a manservant or maidservant, he must let the servant go free to compensate for the tooth. (Exodus 21:23–27)

While this sounds rather brutal, it was very restrained and mild in comparison to the nations around. They usually lived by a harsher code, where death was meted out for the most trivial of offences, and usually not just to the offender, but to all those connected with them, in order to discourage other offenders. Comparing the lives of children in Sparta[1] (Ancient Greece) with those of children in Israel shows how humanitarian and caring the rules in Israel were. Again, there would be exceptions in Israel's history, but the expectations of God's rules were very unusually humanitarian. We need to reconsider our use of discipline today. How far down the line of severity is it right to go in order to reflect the teaching of the Bible in regard to the raising of children?

God's policy on punishments was that they were always for specific purposes, to correct wrongful behaviour and teach the child the right way of living. Punishment was necessary, because the person's behaviour was vitally important.

The Bible also gives us an interesting motivation for punishment: that of love. The motivation to punish must reflect the sort of statement that parents make – 'This will hurt me more than it hurts you' – just before administering a punishment. It is a statement the child never really understands, until becoming a parent in their turn. Punishment must be painful for a parent to inflict, for it has to be rooted in a deep love for the child, but with recognition that the punishment is necessary to help the child. It is the right attitude of the parent which seems to be crucial here. It is to reflect God's attitudes once again. Punishment out of anger is clearly not part of God's plan, and he doesn't excuse it.

The Jewish pattern caused parents to keep a close eye on standards in the home–learning what God wanted them to be, and then applying them. They were not to let them slip, but had to apply discipline whenever necessary to maintain that standard. These are areas woefully lacking in many homes today. We have all seen the example of the child in the supermarket really giving his parent a hard time. The desperate

---

2   I. Smale, *A History of Children*, pp. 33–45.

parent threatens the child wildly, but never actually *does* anything, and the child knows it, and does not stop. There are no absolute standards of right and wrong, and no boundaries that the child cannot pass. The problem of a lack of respect and personal responsibility in our modern generation arises from this sort of parenting attitude. Is it surprising when we allow our children to learn that there is no ultimate law, and that there are no absolutes? Here the Jewish system had no problems, for there were standards and absolutes, and everyone knew what they were.

## 3. What was a family?

'Then all the people left, each for his own home, and David returned home to bless his family' (1 Chronicles 16:43). To understand the family a little better we need to take off our twenty-first century spectacles and step back into ancient Near Eastern society. In Old Testament times men and women were seen in a very different light to the way they are today. It is often the view that women were seen as second best in Jewish culture, but this is misguided. It is true that women did not have the equality we would wish to see today, but they did have a clearly defined role that was very different from that of the men. They also had, within the Jewish culture, more freedom and respect accorded them than other contemporary cultures, where they were often little more than mere slaves or, worse still, items of furniture to be bought and sold.

### (a) The mother

The model wife is described for us in Proverbs 31:10–31. There the Bible holds up for us God's ideal pattern. She seeks the best for her family, whether it is in food or material possessions. She works hard and can put her hand to many tasks. She looks forward to the future, knowing her family is well provided for. She is wise, charitable and dignified. She is well respected both by members of her family and by those outside it. In short she is Supermum! The Bible really has a very high expectation of mothers.

On top of all that, the family would most probably own some land. The wife would have her own responsibilities to fulfil there, and her children were expected to help her in them. Her primary role then was to support her husband in all that they did together as parents, workers, and members of the community. That meant raising a family as much as it meant raising corn or chickens.

The biblical picture of husband and wife shows them to be one unit, one flesh. The wife had a very important role, being the backbone of the family, the central pillar around which everything hung. The husband was perhaps more the planner and visionary. If the wife held the tents and flocks together, the husband knew where to pitch them, and how to get on with the neighbour. It was a joint operation, with both in important and complementary roles.

When planning a family, both husband and wife had to be prepared to take the responsibility very seriously, and become personally involved in the spiritual, physical and moral upbringing of their child. The parenting responsibility and spiritual care of the child began at birth. At this stage, the baby was primarily in the care of the mother. She was responsible for the feeding and daily care, though the parents together shared in responsibility for the raising of the child. It was the sort of sharing where, practically speaking, the mum did all the work and the dad supervised. This pattern, incidentally, has nothing to support it textually; the Bible does not talk of the problem of breast-feeding, night feeds, and a husband who goes off to work, or of working mothers. The problems of our society are a million miles away from the simplicity (if hardship) of those days. Trying to support the notion that the biblical pattern states that mothers should remain home to look after their offspring is suspiciously convenient for the male population. It probably has little to do with the actual commands of God, but more to do with the way society operated in those days.

The mother also grew in status in the community when she gave birth to a son as this helped perpetuate the family line, something of immense significance to the Israelites (as it was in other cultures around them). It is true that most of the passages relating to parenting in the Bible relate to the father, for his role as head of the household was very important, but certainly initially the influence of the mother was very strong. She remained important throughout her children's lives. In fact, the role of the Jewish mother is practically proverbial.

Her role with the daughters was more important still, because she took a strong hand in their education. Her responsibility under God in that society remained in the home, giving a good witness there, organising and running things smoothly and efficiently in accordance with all God's principles. Israel was supposed to meet with God as much in the home as in the market place, or the temple. The mother was particularly important in this (see Deuteronomy 6:7).

The mother had a great deal to do with the upbringing of the child, both physically and spiritually, as Proverbs illustrates: 'Listen, my son, to your father's instruction and do not forsake your mother's teaching' (Proverbs 1:8).

## (b) The father

The father's main responsibility was to care for his family as head of the household. There are few direct references to this

responsibility; it rather runs through the whole of ancient
society as an unwritten assumption. Job 1:1–5, however, is a
clear example of a father who is the head of his house and
family. Another and perhaps supreme example of a father's
control over the destiny of his children is Abraham in Genesis
22:1–14, where he takes his firstborn son Isaac and is ready to
kill him in response to God's commands. He knew that even
should he kill Isaac, then God would restore him, as Hebrews
11:19 makes clear. Yet still he makes the decision to kill Isaac.
Sarah is not mentioned in the process at all. We cannot
imagine a scenario in which she was *not* consulted; merely
that ultimately the decision (and responsibilities) rested
primarily with Abraham as the head of the house.

So the father remains ultimately responsible for the children and their spiritual development. That particular
responsibility came upon the man, according to Genesis 3:16,
as a result of the fall. Because it was part of the curse after the
fall, God knew that this would be difficult to work out in
practice; and relationships and roles would be a strain
between man and woman. Nonetheless, this pattern of roles
remains, whether the couple will accept it or not. The
husband has an awesome responsibility, which Paul points
out in Ephesians 5:25. The husband needs to devise ways and
means of keeping a close watch on, and taking helpful action
in, the physical and spiritual development of the child. For
fathers today, this is often difficult. Work takes so much time
and energy in many careers, that the father rarely spends
much time with his children. In fact, the father figure has
even entered our language as a threat in the phrase 'Wait till
your father gets home' as an exasperated mother reaches her
wits' end. This is not how it was meant to be in God's design,
but modern society is shaping us this way.

Carrying ultimate responsibility as a loving role model of

God's wisdom, love and justice, shaping and directing the spiritual development of his family and home life, the father is an awesome model to aspire to, as was the role of mother above.

## (c) The wider family

It is clear from Proverbs 1:8 that both the father and mother were responsible for bringing up their children as God wished. That was the pattern God had made for the development of children, but in the Law God also made allowances for the family where one or both of the children's parents were missing (through death or divorce). Then, in verses like Deuteronomy 14:29, the wider family were obligated to help care (in its widest sense) for the children, as well as for the widow where relevant. Then aunts, uncles and older cousins, as well as the grandparents, assumed more responsibility for the development and support of the children.

It was not only in this case that the wider family was involved, however; they also had a permanent responsibility for the care of the children in all families. It was not as strong as that of the parents' responsibilities, but it was nevertheless very real. A hypothetical Uncle Esau and Auntie Hannah would often see their nephews and nieces, have them round, and let them play with their cousins. They would, after all, only live next door, or at least very locally. When the children played together, they would be playing under the same rules from one household to the next. Each household was still under the authority of the grandfather, enabling a uniformity of standard, which was intended to be God's standard. All the families would love the same God, and live by the same absolute standard – God's Law (though admittedly Israel was not as faithful to these rules as God would have liked).

These days, as parents we have to be careful where our children play, and also who they play with, for there are so many standards and approaches to life. We have to draw the line when children complain 'But so and so does it, goes there, has seen it' etc. Having a wider family where the standards were the same, and the message going to the children was the same, was very helpful. Children were supposed to see and follow a single example and pattern from all their role models. It is sad that it is very different today, but this appears to be the price Christians pay for being in the world but not of it.

The wider family was, as a supplement to the parents, also responsible for teaching the children about God. Deuteronomy 6:4–9 suggests that the children should learn about God at home and throughout the rest of the day too in the company of their friends and relatives in the small tribal or village community. This teaching about living with God wasn't supposed to be reserved for the sabbath. They were meant to live, drink, eat and breathe it all through the week in every place they worked, learned or played, and with whoever they were in the company of.

Today, we need a safe, wider family like this for our children to play in. The church community can provide that. Yet there are dangers too in isolating the children from the world and its pressures. Being naïve is poor protection from the modern world. So while this wider family concept is helpful, it is dangerous to take too far. But how far is too far?

## 4. The way of wisdom

'Listen, my son, to your father's instruction and do not forsake your mother's teaching' (Proverbs 1:8). The children were taught wisdom in a way that is very different from modern concepts. Today we think of GCSEs, BTECs, 'A' levels and degrees. Ancient Israel had a much more pragmatic view of wisdom. The only real criterion to judge the value of any particular piece of wisdom was the question 'Does it work?' The parents and wider family taught the children the wisdom of the generations by both precept and example. A wise person, in the eyes of the Jews, was one who had been through a lot of experiences, learned the best way of coping with life, and was able to pass those lessons on. In God's Law, the best way of coping with life was defined as 'the way God wants it to be'. God set the agenda, and showed his people how to live, and in return promised to be their God and care for and provide for them. The book of Proverbs is full of this sort of approach to wisdom. Experience was the great teacher, and so the parents were meant to pass on the experiences of their lives to their children so that they could avoid the same mistakes. This is an important part of the parental role, and is mentioned quite frequently in Proverbs particularly: 'Now then, my sons, listen to me; do not turn aside from what I say' (Proverbs 5:7; see also Proverbs 4:1 or Proverbs 7:24).

However, God's way of wisdom had a special edge to it, because it related specifically, as everything else in their lives, to their worship of Yahweh. The parent had to teach the child the wisdom of God, which was defined as the best way to live their lives in order to please God.

The wisdom to be instilled into a child was not only about acceptable behaviour but also about godly living (see Proverbs 1:7). What is really peculiar is the way the Bible talks about a parent who achieves this. Such a parent is described as having served his nation and done his part in maintaining the covenant that God has made, for the next generation. Israel felt that the children must remain loyal to the covenant with God for the sake of the future of the nation. It is a requirement of being a good parent to raise your children in covenant obedience, so the work of God can continue down the centuries.

There was a great sense of continuity in the people. God felt that Israel, whom he described as 'my children', must learn of God in order to pass on the great traditions. This idea of 'passing on the family traditions' used to be important to us, but is not really so any longer. The days when little Johnny simply *had* to be a butcher or baker (or whatever) like his dad are going fast. In fact little Johnny is likely to choose a world philosophy directly opposed to that of his parents. These are the days of rebellion against what the parents do. For ancient Israel though it was essential that their children learned to trust God and continue the great traditions of the past. The Talmud[3] says, 'He who withholds a lesson from his pupils robs him of the heritage of his father.'

This training would begin immediately, though at first the child would not be aware of it. From their earliest days children were surrounded by things their parents did that assumed the existence and relevance of God. The whole lifestyle of the child was focused around God and living for God. It was a subtle form of teaching, where the values and ideology were lived and breathed. In comparison, our own parenting of children has often got too many and varied influences and we give the children a confused message where God is not as important as other issues are.

The children did not learn alternative ideas or ways of thinking and behaving, unlike today's society, where there are multiple lifestyles and belief systems available. All of this teaching was based on the experience of their parents, and before them of the grandparents, who in turn learned much from their own forebears. It was always the same in ancient

---

3   The Talmud is a collection of the teachings of Jewish rabbis.

Israel. That was fine for a non-changing society, but clearly that has difficulties for today's flexible and ever changing world.

## 5. Child development in Israel

'Remember your Creator in the days of your youth' (Ecclesiastes 12:1).

### (a) Early stages

*(i) Circumcision*   Moving forward a few days in the child's development after the birth, the next big day was circumcision when they were eight days old. Again the Bible focuses on the male child here (it being circumcision), but the females also shared in the naming ceremony that usually followed circumcision. The boy was taken to the priest or temple in obedience to an ancient covenant given by God to Abraham in Genesis 17:11. To be circumcised meant that the child was to be thought of as the future part of the nation of Israel, God's special people. As the boy grew, the sign of his circumcision would be a continual reminder to him that he was part of God's chosen people. The sign was in an important place, in an area sensitive and precious, to show that he was to share such sensitive and private things with God. It was also in a place where he would be reminded of the covenant with God several times each day – each time he went to the toilet for instance. As he grew, the child had a constant reminder that God thought he was special, and his parents thought God was special, to have undergone this painful ceremony with him. This idea of self-worth, and of there being someone who thinks you special, is an important issue for today's generation.

*(ii) The naming*   Following this ceremony was the naming, where the parents named the child before God. The name was usually connected to God in some way, either by his actions, e.g. Moses (drawn from the water – Exodus 2:10) or as a statement of his character, e.g. Daniel (God is judge). The name was meant to be an expression of the parents' hope for the child, or perhaps the prophetic outworking of God's plans in the child. For example, Genesis 4:25 mentions Eve naming Seth, which means 'replacement'. We do the same today, with girls called Holly or boys called Noel or even Christmas (usually quickly shortened to Kit). They relate to the time of our birth. Or possibly they echo the name of a parent or another member of the family, so some strange and old-fashioned name gets wished upon some poor unsuspecting child. Or parents give their children names relating to the dreams they hold, calling them after an entire football team, or a pop star, or soap actress. We visit some terrible things on our children when we name them. In Israel, the hopes and expectations were all based around God, and so the names reflected this. The child then had spiritual expectations (rather than our sporting, or acting expectations) set upon them, which the parents had to work to maintain, and God in his control of history worked out.

While seeking to encourage your child towards a real faith in God is definitely what God expects, over-strong parental expectations can also be a pressure for the child, whether it's to become a golfing sensation, or a spiritual giant. It is not healthy for parents to try to live out their ambitions through the lives of their children.

*(iii) Redeemed children*   In addition to this, Exodus 13:2 tells the parents that if their new baby boy was their first male child then they had to 'redeem' him from God when he was a

month old. To redeem means 'to get release by paying something'. His parents therefore had to give God a gift of money to buy their parental rights for this child. The Israelites believed that all the firstborn especially belonged to God. This came originally from the time when God had spared the firstborn sons of Israel during the plagues in Egypt. So ever since then, the parents had to 'redeem' the firstborn (who should have died in Egypt in that plague) by paying five shekels of silver to the priestly treasury. When the tax was paid, the boy was considered 'redeemed' from God, and belonged to the family once more. This all meant that the family had to value the child. Paying five shekels of silver (a substantial amount) helped the parents to realise that the child really was important. He was not just a 'thing' they could dispose of as they wished, like other societies around did, selling their children into slavery if they were poor, or killing them in an offering to idols. Israelite parents really had to encourage this child to follow God and love God for himself. This child, being firstborn (and male, in Israel's society), would then become the family head of the tribe for the next generation, and hopefully he would love God for himself, thus carrying the faith forward.

Perhaps we need to look again at the way we value children, in society, the home, and also in the church or class groups that we are part of.

*(iv) Weaning*   The next significant event in the life of the child was weaning. Babies were not usually weaned from breast milk until two or even three years old. This meant that the children were very closely linked to the mother for a much longer period of time than is true of modern Western society, and a strong bond was formed.

Weaning was also marked by a major family celebration.

Abraham made a great feast when Isaac was weaned in Genesis 21:8. It was another landmark in the maturity of the child and another stage the child had survived. The child was more likely to grow into an adult now and the terrible infant mortality rate would not claim another victim. The child was no longer a baby, but not yet an adult. With the development beyond baby stage came a new stimulus and input for the children. From this point on, the children were encouraged to go to the three annual festivals in Israel. Until this age, they did not usually go, for very practical reasons, as the festivals were usually held at distant places, and travelling with an infant is a major task in any period of history. Once children were weaned, travel for the mother and child was easier, and children took their place in the wider society of Israel, through the festivals particularly. We will look at these festivals in more detail in the next chapter, and how they were designed to teach and encourage the faith of people of all ages, not merely the adults. What is particularly noteworthy, though, is that this socialising in Israelite terms included public worship. Not merely mother and toddler groups, but full-blown worship services.

## (b) Education in general

With the passing of the weaning stage, the child moved on another major step towards adulthood. This involved new responsibilities for the child. At home the mother and father started to teach them their first lessons. While this would have included their ABC (or their Aleph, Beth and Gimel in Hebrew) this was not the priority that it is in today's society. These early lessons were more practical, and took place while the parents were going about their daily business. The child learned by example, doing what the parents were doing. They learned the necessary skills from their parents by helping in the fields, workshops or kitchen as soon as they could walk. This almost certainly meant that they were a real hindrance and hassle to their parents at first, but through this apprenticeship, real skills soon started to emerge (as well as real disasters from time to time, certainly). Education was about life-skills rather than anything more abstract. The child learned how to handle the real disasters, as well as the real triumphs of success.

Modern educationalists consider that the best way to learn is to see and do, and this is the method of education God suggested. The child was with the parents, both seeing and doing all day long, learning what they did, how they did it, and most importantly why they did it that way. A lot of what was learned was practical, particularly relating to the trade the father practised. Alongside all that, though, came morals and motivations, all based round a worldview that directed and drove the father; the 'why' of the work that was being done. In Israel that worldview was designed to please God. The father would be a farmer, or a carpenter, doing things a certain way because he was doing them for God. It is possible to make a table or chair for God. The values of honesty, care and love being put into the object would show morals, but also the value that God placed on us in making us.

The child then caught his father's godly values unconsciously. They would be absorbed rather than directly taught. The child would be trained by experience and a thousand practical examples rather than by rote. Western society is completely different. We feel that education is the job of the state, which will prepare the country's children for life, both in terms of vocational training and in moral and religious teaching. This has led to an abdication by many parents of the education role, and a failure to be role models for the children. The state will not, by determined act, teach them the morals or values of God. It will teach facts but no moral framework into which the facts fit. For example, children are supposed to learn all the facts about sex and the dangers of unprotected sex, but not about the moral dimensions of relationships, let alone the spiritual ones. They are taught instead that there are no absolute states of right or wrong, and that everyone needs to find their own values within themselves. It is not surprising to see where that has led us.

God is therefore suggesting that we have a moral framework for the education of our children, and that it should be his morals, lived out and taught by the family, and especially the parents. The facts should be given, but with some idea of what should be done with those facts.

*(i) Parental education: before God*    Deuteronomy 6:4–9 suggests that children should learn about God at home. This was considered to be a very serious responsibility for the parents. God taught Israel that if their faith were to continue through the rest of history, it had to be taught correctly to their children, and the responsibility lay fully with them. As we have seen, in every aspect of life the parents would talk about God, and the children would learn in very practical and real ways the importance of following him. This was a lifelong commitment from the parent to the child, starting from birth.

This is a very different approach to children from that of our society, which puts children in front of the TV, gets nannies and day nurseries to care for the pre-schooler, then has after-school clubs and latch-key clubs for those old enough to go to school. Modern society, while needing these things because of its pressures, is perhaps abandoning its children to the care of society rather than the parent. It is a real question for us to address. This means that rather than learning the values of God through the parents, the children learn their facts, but put them into a framework provided by other people, who may not love and honour God as your children need.

God arranged things so that the lives of the parents trained the children in the values of living with God and the reality of living with God. This, if followed properly, was far more powerful than a hundred synagogue services, or lectures on morality. God knew this, and encouraged Abraham to do it (see Genesis 18:19).

*(ii) Parental education: prayer*  The parents' work and responsibilities began with prayer. They had an obligation to pray for their children; that they would follow the Lord, or that the parents themselves would be good parents, and treat their children properly in a way that would encourage faith.

There are many examples of Old Testament saints praying earnestly for their families and children. They include Manoah praying for his child Samson in Judges 13, Hannah praying for a son in 1 Samuel 1:11, and Abraham's servant, who was praying for a wife for Isaac in Genesis 24:44. There are examples of the wider village community praying earnestly, even prophetically, for a certain child who would be born, as in Ruth 4:11–12. The most detailed example is that of Job in chapter 1 verse 5. After a great family celebration, on the off-chance that one of them had gone away from the Lord and forgotten God in the excitement of the party, Job arose early to pray. His prayers also included sacrifices for each child at great personal cost, both financially and in time. Job is held up as the great example of the family man in the first chapter, a model for us to follow. He is a wealthy famous business tycoon in the haulage business (camels) and farming world (cows and donkeys). Yet it does not stop him taking all this time out very early in the morning (and remember he is a farmer, when early means early) and praying for his children individually each time his family meets. He prays and sacrifices for each one individually, and as he has ten children, it must take some considerable time and cost. He does this merely as a precaution. There is no certainty of their sinning here, or of failure; he is simply very concerned for each of his children individually. The word 'cursed' that the NIV uses is perhaps an over-translation of the Hebrew, which might merely suggest forgetfulness for a period. Therefore Job was not praying out of desperation for his wayward children, which is when we are usually driven to prayer, but regularly out of concern for children who are displaying faith.

They would also have to teach their children how to pray for themselves. That would begin with mimicry, the children copying what they heard their parents speak in prayer, before developing a real prayer life of their own. While we do not have any specific examples to point to for this practice, it is absolutely in line with the way the Israelites taught their children everything. In applying this we need to think of the sort of long-winded prayers full of theological terms that tend to dominate our prayer meetings and church services. It is difficult to think of our children understanding them, let alone copying them. Perhaps we need to change our approach a little sometimes.

*(iii) Parental education: the importance of an example*
Another responsibility the parents faced was of maintaining a close family fellowship, and time when the parent and child together would share in worshipping God. In its more formal nature, this is going to be discussed in the next chapter, but there is an informal sense as well, when the parents would worship with their children privately, outside of the set feasts

and fasts. We don't have many examples of this in Scripture, because it is not the main focus of the passages, but it is clearly part of the important role that the parents had in training their children to follow in their example. There is one good example of this, however, in the relationship that Abraham had with Isaac. They go off together to worship God privately. It is a painful journey, for this is where Abraham thinks that he is going to sacrifice his son, according to God's clear command. Yet as far as Isaac is concerned, the two are off on retreat together. This is a time for the father and son to pray together. As the son learned everything else from his father by example, so here the son learns how to pray, and meet with God: 'He said to his servants, "Stay here with the donkey while I and the boy go over there. We will worship and then we will come back to you"' (Genesis 22:5).

This is also seen in the way the children were encouraged to talk to God personally twice a day (and with respect and honour), though they could not see him. They had seen their parents praying, and copied the parents' attitude and habits. The Jews were encouraged to make sacrifices to God twice a day, morning and evening (mentioned in Ezra 3:3 for example). The parents then prayed twice daily, and would involve the family in the sacrifice, and presumably therefore also in their prayers. As the children grew, their parents, who had been praying with them, now started to encourage them to do so for themselves. More importantly, the children could also see their parents and wider family giving God the same respect that they were being asked to give. It became natural for them to do the same.

While books on parenting these days tend to push the importance of spending time with the children – quality time, on a one-to-one basis – and often recommend a trip to McDonald's with a single child and single parent, this is not really enough. Admittedly, they are right, and spending time together is essential, but it is merely the beginning. It is also important that this is built on, and the child sees a real and living faith in the parents, in everything that is done.

*(iv) Parental education: the laws of God*    A further responsibility of the parents was to teach their children the laws of God. The children were expected to learn sections of the Scriptures by heart. Particularly in the evenings, when all the work was done and before going to bed, members of the family would recite many of the stories now written down in the Bible. Obviously, with none of our modern entertainment, this meant sitting down and talking together, relating these stories and experiences of God. This worked well with them, but appears to be very difficult in our generation and society. We have to consider ways in which we can make this time of reflecting on God together meaningful within our own lifestyle, learning the stories of his goodness, both from the Bible and also our own lives. This is of course not easy, and there is no magic fix. The children had to take their turns in this family time of devotion and worship of God. Getting the children actually to participate was and is the best way of encouraging them in the ways of God. This pattern of continual instruction in the 'ways of God' continued throughout all the stages of the child's day. Deuteronomy commands the parents:

> Impress them on your children. Talk about them when you sit at home and when you walk along the road, when you lie down and when you get up. (Deuteronomy 6:7)

Such guidance should be positive, by both example and precept, aiming to 'Train a child in the way he should go, and when he is old he will not turn from it' (Proverbs 22:6). The aim of all this teaching of the children by the parents is clear from Deuteronomy:

> Their children, who do not know this law, must hear it and learn to fear the LORD your God as long as you live in the land you are crossing the Jordan to possess. (Deuteronomy 31:13)

It was to make the children fear and love the Lord for themselves, and to personally accept and walk in the ways of God, and acknowledge the covenant with God in their own lives. The cumulative effect of the family living for God was designed to have a very positive impact on the child. This is even more important these days, due to the negative impact that secular society has. Ancient Israel did not have to worry about the educational value of secular society, or have to re-educate their children to their own values. We do, and so the parental influence and bond needs to be all the stronger if we are to draw our children closer to God.

*(v) Learning the Law*   As the child grew, so did their need to understand and learn the Scriptures. This was a further responsibility of the parents. Throughout their childhood, children were actively encouraged to learn portions of the Torah (the first five books of the Bible) by heart. This was so they would remember the laws of God for themselves, and start to learn to apply them to their own lives. The children were learning that God was relevant and important from his actions, and now they learned by heart what God wanted from them in return. It was a practical linking of God's laws and their daily lives. From the first days that the child learned to read, the parents were responsible for their child's theological education. Leviticus was the first book they studied.

While this probably comes as a major surprise to us, it is actually very sensible. Leviticus is a very visual book, which makes it easier for young children to grasp. It does not, at its most basic level, need any abstract ideas, but can all be concrete and visual, acting out the responsibilities that people have towards God. The sacrificial system was a very visual and dramatic experience, which made a strong impact on children.[4] The rest of the book of Leviticus deals with practical and relevant details about God, and what he wants us to be. They are very down to earth and relevant (provided you see them through an ancient Israelite's eyes). This emphasis on Leviticus as a beginning showed the importance that the Jews placed on teaching the children about living pure lives, even while they were still fairly young. This lifestyle was designed to give them a better basis for living, not only as a member of the family as we would see it, but as a member of God's people too.

*(vi) Remembering the Law*   A further part of the instruction that the Jewish children received would have come from the tefillin[5] their fathers wore. They were bound on the arm in such a way as to create a shape like the English letter W (actually the Hebrew letter 'shin'), the first letter of 'Shaddai', meaning 'Almighty'. Such outward acts would prompt the child's curiosity as to why his parent was doing this, and then he would be impressed by the seriousness, and the real-ness of their faith in God. This was paralleled by the Mezuzah, which

---

4   I have used the sacrificial system in Leviticus in my own teaching among both churched and unchurched children with significant response.

5   These were small boxes of texts from the Torah (the first five books of the Bible) that had to be memorised, and which the adult tied around his forearm, and upon his forehead.

the child would also see every time he went in and out of the house. This was another box with texts in, fixed to the doorpost of the house, immediately visible every time the child went through the door. These are still used today in the homes of many Orthodox Jews. If you enter their homes today, you will see these small boxes on the doorposts. There is a little window in the box, and the text inside is arranged so that the word 'Almighty' is visible. In ancient Israel (and still today), each time the parents passed, they would touch this little window with a finger, kiss that finger, and offer a benediction. It was a powerful image that the children would naturally start to imitate for themselves, thus making them start to pray, and revere the Almighty.

So the family home and environment was designed to teach children all they would need to know for life, and bound up in it were lessons of theology as well as lessons about earning a living and personal care. Their religion, which was taught by example and history, was learned through stories and by question and answer, and memorised.

## (c) Rebellious children

Children were not always amenable (and have not changed) to their parents' teaching, despite the most godly and caring instruction and example. There are no guarantees in the Bible that the child will automatically respond even to the best and most biblical parenting. The Bible mentions many godly people whose sons and daughters (in the context of the biblical narrative they are more usually sons) do not follow in their ways. Aaron's sons, Eli's sons, and Samuel's sons are all cases in point. Samson is perhaps the best known example of a wayward child in the Bible, despite all the benefits and blessings of God. The story of the line of the kings of Judah is also littered with examples through the books of 1 and 2

Kings. Children obedient to the laws of God and their parents in fact appear to be the exception rather than the rule.

The New Testament makes the children's behaviour a test for eldership (see Titus 1:6), thinking that if a man can show a good and consistent example at home, and his children respond to it, he is likely to be a good elder.

Admittedly, sometimes the parents in the Bible are examples of how *not* to go about God's laws, but the examples mentioned above are of godly parents. So while the waywardness of our children could have something to do with an inconsistency in our parenting, rebellion can happen in even the godliest home. We must do the best we can do for our children. Sometimes, being individuals with their own minds, they just choose their own paths, which do not include the God we serve. Perhaps you might need to take comfort from that if things are not well at home despite your best efforts, and God hasn't convicted you of things that you might have done differently.

### (d) Rebellious parents

Coupled with this, there are also fearful warnings in the book of Jeremiah about parents who fail even to try to fulfil their parenting role. Parenting is a terrible responsibility. Jeremiah seems harsh in this respect when he says:

> Why should I forgive you? Your children have forsaken me and sworn by gods that are not gods. I supplied all their needs, yet they committed adultery and thronged to the houses of prostitutes. (Jeremiah 5:7)

It seems to imply that a parent who cannot be bothered to try and raise their children by God's standards cannot expect mercy and forgiveness from God for themselves. It is very difficult to accept such a harsh statement, and take its implications on board, applying it to our families and our churches. Yet the scripture reveals God's mind in this, and is clear. We are the ones with a difficulty here.

## (e) Developing education

As the child grew, from his earliest years and throughout childhood, God planned for there to be a great unchanging routine of family worship, and public worship with their family. God would have been constantly treated as a real person to be spoken to, and whose word was to be obeyed even by the parents. This God was also to be worshipped in big festivals, which were exciting and had real relevance to the child. There the child realised that everyone did this, that there were thousands of other people worshipping this God too, and that everything was perfectly right and normal.

As life went on, the children should have been encouraged to pray twice daily, hear others pray, recognise God's activity in response to those prayers, see his love and care, and try to live in obedience to God's commands. The home was the focus for all that the children learned. If children were to learn successfully, then they needed to see God honoured genuinely in the home, on good days and bad ones. They needed to know that God was real and relevant in all aspects of their lives, and cared about how they lived on a daily basis. Leviticus contains a lot of commands about daily living, developing their education as the child grew and encountered new life issues. The way in which this lifestyle was actually lived out would really teach the child about the reality and relevance of faith in God.

Israelite society was designed so that God pervaded every part of their weekly and yearly cycle. This meant that God just kept cropping up in conversation. Their history was also a continual object lesson from which the children could learn. The book of Joel makes the point when it says, 'Tell it to your children, and let your children tell it to their children, and their children to the next generation' (Joel 1:3).

## (f) Reaching maturity

From this point on, the child grew and developed with God and his parents until such time as he was considered to be mature. This raises the question of the age of maturity in Israel, when the parents were no longer held responsible for the child's actions. Exactly when this occurred is (as we have seen) difficult to determine, and probably it happened at different times as the society developed over centuries. One such possible date for this was the coming of age ceremony. This appears to have related to the age of twelve or thirteen. From this point on, children (particularly females) were reaching adulthood and could soon be married. At some points in history, the age of maturity was measured by the appearance of two body hairs on a boy (a measure of the age of puberty). So it appears that the word 'children' in the Old Testament relates principally to those from infancy to maturity at the age of twelve or thirteen. It is easier to see the spiritual effect of these changes in boys than it is in girls from the Bible, because of the nature of the Old Testament record. The boy at this age officially became 'a son of the Law', and had to take on the responsibilities of keeping the Law. He was allowed to wear the tefillin and could be counted as one of the ten necessary male adults who were needed if the Jews were to have a time of public prayer. He was also eligible for being 'called up' in the synagogue to read the whole or a portion of the Torah for that day, or to lead the synagogue in prayers. From the point of view of Jewish religious law, he was treated as an adult with all the duties and privileges.

From the following day, he was expected to observe all the relevant commandments and to be responsible for his own behaviour. It is perhaps difficult to imagine such a responsibility being given to pre-teenagers in our churches today. Indeed, even when they are, there is usually an 'aaah' factor involved, and the children often get a round of applause for performing, when actually they are only bringing their worship to God in the same way an adult would. Sadly we often patronise them and treat their worship as a 'performance'.

At this point, the child moves out of the scope of this book. Today such a child would be called a 'teenager' and moves outside the scope of children's work, if not actually outside of the entire human race for a few years! This does not mean that parents from this point cut all their ties with their children. The story of Eli well illustrates that his son's disobedience was still being considered to be partly his responsibility (see 1 Samuel 2:22–25, 31–35). This is true even though they were now priests, and hence were surely considered to be adults. So, once a parent always a parent, and the care of your children in one sense will always be there, though when they reach adult status your responsibility and control diminishes progressively, until ultimately they assume responsibility for themselves.

# 5

# *The Role of Children in Public Worship*

Israel's worship was given to us as a pattern by God, and was designed as an experience in which everyone could share. Psalm 148:12 mentions 'young men, and maidens; old men and children' all involved in worship. It was designed to be a corporate affair for all the family.

In Israel, public worship was all-important and considered compulsory, but there are several types of public worship that we need to explore to see how children were involved in this formal and semi-compulsory worship. There were the times of regular weekly worship, and then also the highlights of the year, at the great annual festivals. Then at special times in the family's history other worship ceremonies took place. In terms of activities, it was rather like church life today.

In Israel, there was a definite sense of the importance of gathering together in these times of worship. We will begin with the great annual festivals before considering the special occasions, and finally going on to the regular weekly worship experience.

## 1. The great festivals

'Three times a year all your men are to appear before the Sovereign LORD, the God of Israel' (Exodus 34:23). Meeting together at the great annual festivals had always been a command of God. However, as we have said, this was not just a time for the men of Israel, it was for the whole people. In fact, as the history of Israel lengthened, new festivals were added to the initial three, commemorating great events that took place (for example the feasts of Purim and Hanukkah). At up to five times in the year, then, the public worship of Israel touched a child's life. There was a cycle of festivals running throughout the year, each having its special emphasis, which we will consider below.

### (a) General points

While these festivals were for all the family, they were certainly very exciting for the children. Every festival had a large symbolic and visual impact, and the children were encouraged to ask what was happening and why, whereupon the parents were expected to explain God's goodness to the children (see for example Exodus 12:25–27). The children learned important information about God right from the beginning.

These sacrifices were very important for another reason, which would escape our notice in modern Western society. In ancient Israel, families would eat red meat only very occasionally. One of those times would have been at these sacrificial occasions. This marked the day as a special one for the children, where they had a special meal that God had provided for them (the animal went to God, who took it, and returned some meat for them to eat). Feast days really were a feast, a real contrast to the many normal days that would see the family going to bed at least a little hungry. This is something that we miss the relevance of in our society where there is always plenty, and obesity is a problem, not a sign of great wealth (which it was then). So a second thing to learn is that the festivals affected the lives of families and children in a very practical way.

The festival times were exciting times for the children, as the families were actually instructed by God to celebrate in an extravagant way. It was meant to be 'party time'. The Bible gives special instructions to the people when they are going to celebrate God in the festivals:

> Use the silver to buy whatever you like: cattle, sheep, wine or other fermented drink, or anything you wish. Then you and your household shall eat there in the presence of the LORD your God and rejoice. (Deuteronomy 14:26)

These instructions related to those who could not take their offerings to the festival because they lived too far away. Then they were to sell the items they would have offered, and buy food or silver with the proceeds, and use it to celebrate with God as a family. God was sanctioning parties at these special times. The children of that society would have been as excited and full of anticipation as children today are before Christmas and Easter.

The celebrations would have begun long before the actual time of the festival, as the people travelled in large groups to the festival.[1] There would have been a party atmosphere the whole way to Jerusalem, with the focus of it being the praise of God.

---

1   Josephus Antiquities 17.313.

*(b) Passover*

The most important festival for Israel was Passover, celebrated at our Easter time in March or April (14th Nisan in the Jewish calendar). It was obligatory, and it celebrated Israel's deliverance from Egypt.

The Passover festival had a special role within the family. It still does today. The family meets, perhaps with friends, for the meal at sun-down of the day before Passover (a new day beginning at this point). The head of the house then gives an opening prayer over the first cup of wine. The group then eats the bitter herbs, which symbolise the bitter times of Israel's history. Then a second cup of wine is poured but not drunk. The main meal is then served, but not eaten until the Passover liturgy is recited. This is widely available in both Hebrew and English and still regularly used. Though today there are varieties of procedure, there is a general agreement over the main features. The entire service is laid out in a handbook for the parents. There is also an edition for children with large print and pictures.

It begins with a son's question to his father: 'How is this night different from all other nights?' The son's instruction is a compulsory and integral part of the feast,[2] and a reminder to all the older children of what they themselves learned as they in their turn had asked the question. This one question naturally gives rise to many more, such as: 'Why is the lamb roasted whole?', 'Why are the herbs bitter?', 'Why is there no yeast?', etc. The family head takes this as his cue to explain the symbolism of the feast as the meal progresses.

Then Psalm 113, the Hallel, herbs is sung, and the main meal is eaten after a prayer over the unleavened bread. A

---

2   I. Smale, *A History of Children*, p. 117.

prayer over the third cup ends the feast. Then Psalms 114 to 118 are sung and a fourth cup of parting is drunk.[3]

For children of ancient Israel this was a special time. A whole lamb would be eaten that night, a rare feast of meat where they had to eat it all! There would be the preparations for the main meal, with special arrangements to be made and a sense of atmosphere about the home. The whole meal itself was carefully structured as a time of teaching the importance of this Passover, and reminding the children what it was that God had done.

Before (or sometimes in the middle of) the feast, there would be the game of 'hunt the yeast'. The father (enthusiastically assisted by the children) searched the house to make sure that there was none left at all, nor any food containing it. The mother beforehand would have cunningly hidden the *afikomen* (half of an unleavened loaf representing the affliction of the Jews) somewhere to be found by the children. The one who found it usually received a small reward.[4] It would be ritual largely, but fun, and above all it would have a teaching element to it, as yeast was the symbol for sin and corruption.

### (c) Firstfruits, or Weeks, or Pentecost (meaning 50 days)

This happened 50 days after Passover. It was to give thanks to God for the grain harvest. The first sheaf of the harvest was taken and given to God (see Leviticus 23:9–11). In other nations this belonged to the king as a tax, but here it was to be given to God, because after all God was their king. Over the years it became quite an organised and ritualistic ceremony, which went something like this.

The day before the first harvest, the actual sheaves were

3   J. A. Thompson, *A Handbook of Life in Bible Times* (IVP, 1986), p. 342.
4   A. Wood, *Judaism*, p. 40.

selected, and tied up, while still growing in the ground. The next day, a crowd would gather to watch. The reaper had particular questions to ask, and the crowd would give their response, before the sheaves were finally harvested and taken off to the priests. They would then offer them to God in cere-mony, thanking God for the harvest. This was a national holiday, and each family produced freshly baked bread from the grain, and a feast in the fields would begin. After this day, the work in the fields began in earnest, where the whole community would stop what they were doing and join in the harvest. This made it a memorable time once more for the children, free from usual activities, bringing in food for the next year, but firmly in the context that all this was from God and the whole community recognised it.[5]

On this day though, while the community would have been very excited about the latest crop, and eager to get it harvested (before the rains came and ruined it), the harvest had to wait, while the most important person, God (not the king), was given his share first. This was the main message of the festival. This was observed in local sanctuaries as well as in Jerusalem, and it was primarily an offering of the firstfruits of the land. The feast became a great pilgrimage to Jerusalem in Josiah's day.[6]

Once again, the first and best was offered to God before Israel could harvest any for their own use. God was their king, and their provider. This was particularly clear in the way that Israel made the offering, at least in later centuries. The wheat was ground into flour and they made bread with it. The loaves though were baked into the shape of an altar, complete with the little horns on each corner where the

5   I. Smale, *A History of Children,* p. 118.
6   J. A. Thompson, *Handbook of Life in Bible Times*, p. 342.

priests made the sacrifices. The bread was therefore a visual aid for the whole community of their entire system of belief, and their hope in God, rather like (but more meaningful than) the special harvest loaves that can be seen shaped like sheaves of wheat in church harvest festivals today.

The whole period was very busy for the family with everyone out in the fields for the harvest, and working late. They would often have slept out together in the fields too (see Ruth 3). Harvest times have always been times of excitement and partying for the societies that have been close to agriculture, and this would certainly have been true of Israel, with the added dimension that God was the centre of all the partying.

This has not changed today, for in modern Israel children and young adults still play an active role in the ceremonies, involving song and dance as well as the collection of harvest goods for distribution.[7]

## (d) The Feast of Tabernacles

This was the most popular and joyful of all the festivals. It came at the end of September, and marked another harvest period in Israel's year (see Deuteronomy 16:13–17). It was the end of the grape harvest, when the entire crop had been finally gathered in. It marked the end of the year in terms of agriculture, rather as harvest festivals do today. Originally the people would have lived in the fields to complete their work, in little shelters or booths. In later centuries this practice was continued even though the community was not so agriculturally based. This is because there was also an important symbolism in living in these huts. For seven days they camped out in shelters made from tree branches to commemorate

---

7   A. Wood, *Judaism*, p. 51.

Israel's journey through the desert.[8]

The whole festival was a celebration of God's care and protection over them. First, this year had gone by and God had provided once more. Beyond that, though, there was a lengthy history of God providing. The festival particularly remembered the time in the wilderness when God had provided for them so completely and dramatically. A lot of the symbolism of this festival related to that time. The huts they lived in (and still do today, though more usually now on the balconies of the flats in places like Tel Aviv) were made of willow and myrtle branches. These particular tree branches were chosen in order to remember the weeping and the rejoicing times in the wilderness wanderings. The *sukkah* (temporary hut) lets in rain and wind and, in stormy weather, eating, drinking and maybe sleeping in the *sukkah* can be scary. The *sukkah* shaking and the leafy coverings rustling evoke a feeling of the vulnerability of human nature.[9] Anyone who has camped out with young children can imagine how scary and exciting a time this can be. However, instead of the seemingly obligatory ghost stories, these bedtimes were filled with stories of how God had protected and provided through the centuries, and was still protecting them. This gave a different message altogether. The noise and shaking, the discomfort and worry were all put into the context of trusting God; it would all be OK.

This exciting history was taught to the children as they made the shelters and 'camped out' for a week. The Jews today decorate their shelters with fairy lights and many other bright decorations. In Old Testament times they were also decorated with bright colours and pictures, for the whole

---

8   J. A. Thompson, *Handbook of Life in Bible Times,* pp. 342–3.

9   A. Wood, *Judaism*, p. 55.

period of the feast was planned as a celebration.

The days would have involved worship at the Temple, where the worshippers (children included) were given palm leaves, and myrtle and willow branches to wave (called *lulavs*). These acted as banners and represented shady valleys (where the palm grows), the hillsides and mountains (where the myrtle grows) and the brooks and streams (where the willow grows) that God had led Israel in. They were to bring fruits with them also, probably the citron (a lemony type of fruit), which represented the fruits of this good land that God had given them. Again children would ask why they were doing these things, and were sure to have had great fun during this week of joyful celebration, camping out with their families.[10] It was a carnival occasion. Priests carrying willow branches marched around the altar. There was flute playing and dancing by night.[11] The whole week-long celebration was a party, with joyful dancing, music, and lots of active things that children could do to join in the worship of God, which was the central focus of the festival.

## (e) Day of Atonement

The Feast of Tabernacles finally ended in the Day of Atonement, the great day when the High Priest could go into the Holy of Holies bearing the blood that would atone for the sins of Israel for another year. This is described for us in Leviticus 16, but is mentioned as a special day in Leviticus 23:2. This was another great celebration day, when the sins of the people were removed. Once more there are many details of the day that are extremely visual, and demonstrate clearly the reason for the sacrifice. These include the removal of sins,

---

10 I. Smale, *A History of Children*, p. 121.

11 E. P. Sanders, *Judaism Practice and Belief*, p. 139.

the punishment of the goats and bulls for our sins, the holiness of God, and also the mercy of God, and the reason for the great hope of the people of Israel. Family units were involved together in watching all the elaborate preparations. The children would certainly question, and receive answers for, the very dramatic presentation of God's demands. The people also took the festival and its symbolism very seriously. The Israelites were going to talk to God face to face that day, or at least the High Priest was. Was the High Priest holy enough? Were the sacrifices good enough? If they were not, the High Priest would die! They took this so seriously, according to Jewish traditions, that the High Priest, on going in to the Holy of Holies, would have a rope tied round his ankle so the people could pull his body out if God did strike him dead! All this was dramatic enough to excite every child there.

### (f) Feast of Trumpets

This was the beginning of the New Year, though confusingly it happened in the seventh month, our October. (Read the reference for example in Numbers 29:1–2.) This had to do with their climate and growing season, where they could manage two crops per year. In history, Israel had two alternative views of when the New Year was, and this became the lesser of the two dates, with the Passover marking the other. It was called Trumpets (actually a ram's horn called a *shofar*) because the months and especially years were marked not by calendars, but by the blowing of trumpets. This festival today is called Rosh Hashanah (literally the head of the year). It is a great occasion for the children, where party clothes are worn, and they are given apples cut up and coated with honey to celebrate the hope of a good sweet New Year to come. As it is a New Year, many customs involve renewal and starting again: many have a haircut just before or buy a special outfit. At the very least, all wear their 'best' clothes.[12]

It is another party time, but God is part of it all once more. The synagogue is the focal point, where the *shofar* is blown, and the people are reminded of the Almighty and his place in their year. The story of Isaac is usually taught here too. People are encouraged to consider the past year, and put right all the failures in it, ready to start the New Year afresh with God. It is a lengthy celebration lasting ten days. Modern Western society makes much of the New Year but God is almost always ignored, whereas in the Jewish calendar he is at the centre.

## (g) Purim

There were other festivals added in later centuries as the history of Israel unfolded. Purim is a feast celebrating the rescue of the Jews from destruction during the Persian period (470s BC). Purim means 'lots', and the name refers to the lots cast by Haman, the king's chief minister, to decide on which day he should massacre the Jews (see Esther 3; 7; 9:24, 26). The children acted out the story of Esther, rather like a modern pantomime, and still do today. There is a lot of comedy and drama in the book. They also celebrate it with the sending of gifts (usually via the children) between families. These are usually passed around on the day by personal visit and often in fancy dress for the occasion. The festival is so full of life and action that children naturally enjoy it, and want to know what it is all about. In this way they learn the history of their nation as the people of God. Perhaps this one comes close to our Christmas celebrations.

---

12 A. Wood, *Judaism*, p. 47.

## (h) Hanukkah

This festival commemorated the cleansing and rededication of the second temple by Judas Maccabaeus in 165 BC, after it had been defiled by the Syrian ruler, Antiochus IV Epiphanes. It was also called 'Lights', as each evening lamps were placed in houses and synagogues. This festival, called Dedication in John 10:22, is celebrated today as Hanukkah.

Special candles were burned in people's houses, creating an atmosphere for the children. Then came the dramatic teaching of what happened this time in history, when God did miracles for Israel (1 Maccabees 4:52–59). It is said that God kept the candles burning in the Temple, signifying that he was back with his people, during the time of the re-conquest from the Syrian oppressors, even though the oil for them should have run out.

## Summary

All of these great national festivals had drama, atmosphere and excitement. They were visual, and contained opportunities for the children to talk things through with their parents. In fact they sometimes seem designed to give that very opportunity. This is especially true of Tabernacles perhaps. There is nothing like sitting in a tent through the evening, with your children, to create an opportunity to chat about life, the universe and everything.

We have to ask ourselves what has happened to the church's annual festivals. Have they become stale, rigid and unexciting? Do they engender the sorts of emotions and questions that we see here? This is a challenge to us, as it is to those of the Jewish faith who also have to keep their approach to these festivals alive. These occasions should be a time for all the family, not just the young or the old. The expressions of worship used should reflect this.

## 2. Occasional worship

'When any of you brings an offering to the LORD, bring as
your offering an animal from either the herd or the flock'
(Leviticus 1:2). There were also regular sacrifices to make
throughout the year, depending on the circumstances of a
particular family. These were additional to the other obligations, and incidentally showed the children how important
God was in all that they did. When a family goes to bed
hungry most of the time, the gift of an animal to be
completely burned is a major affair. Yet if that is what the
family chooses to do, then the reason has to be very
important.

### (a) Burnt offering

This was not specifically to do with sin and guilt as we often
think (see Leviticus 1:1–17). It was certainly an opportunity
to say 'hello' to God: 'I love you, and want to approach you,
but cannot without this, because you are a holy God.' Here
God tells us what will make him happy. The details are all
very gruesome to read, but are exactly the sort of thing that
Israel might have expected 3,500 years ago. God asks for a
gift. For Israel here it meant animal sacrifices, because flocks
and herds of animals were practically all Israel had to give.
The details of the passage show us that the gift has to be
precious. It is something valuable, which costs us, not rubbish
that we would throw away anyway. It must also be given
reverently and obediently to God. However, the passage also
shows us that it is to be in proportion to what we have. The
gift is relative to what we can afford. Nobody is excluded
from being able to give, simply because it costs too much.
They are like a child's present to her mother. They are cheap,
tacky, and of no financial value, bought out of dwindling

pocket money, and limited understanding, but they are loved by Mum because of what they mean to her. It really is the thought that counts. The lessons of this sacrifice are important lessons for a child to receive graphically. Practical, and visual, they are easy to understand, whereas an abstract course in the academic theology of offerings would not be. Children can understand that God is great, and holy, but can be approached by those who are prepared to put in the sacrifice and effort.

### (b) Cereal offering

This was a voluntary gift to God, and it was usually an extra offering accompanying either the burnt or the peace offering (see Leviticus 2:1–16; 6:14–23). It was a love gift to God, returned to him, made out of the things he provided us with. Certain ingredients were forbidden in the mixture though. There should be no yeast (Exodus 12:39), which would change the gift, perhaps corrupt it, and also there could be no honey, which might also change the nature of the gift. Both of these things were normal in cooking, but this was special bread, made from the purest and best of God's harvest, and had to be treated differently. The children would have been involved in the home with the making of this, and the special nature of it again would have been the source of comment and questions.

Then the bread was given to the priests, who ate some of it after offering the rest to God. Again this would have fascinated the children, who would have liked a taste, only to be told that they couldn't: it had been given to God and was *corban* (holy). It showed the children something about the priests too. Parents who have had to stop their little ones from eating the communion bread and wine, only to be subjected to a barrage of questions and whining, will know what this must have been like. The important thing is: how do we approach it? As a chance to teach them, or as a chance to silence them?

*(c) Peace offering or thanks offering*

This was a thanks or fellowship offering – again, nothing to do with sin or forgiveness (see Leviticus 3:1–17; 7:11–21). It was the favourite of all the offerings in the Old Testament, appearing often, for example three times in 1 Samuel 1:5, 9 and 24. It is similar to the previous two in that similar goods were to be used, and of similar quality. However, this offering was restricted to certain occasions. When God had been particularly good, and an amazing thing had happened, and you wanted others to know about it, then this was what you did. The animal was sacrificed in the usual way, with the choice parts going to God, to be burned. The rest of the carcass was returned to the worshipper so that he could share a meat feast with his friends and family. They could all marvel together at the Lord's goodness. This would again have an impact on the children, getting a good meal, all in honour of God. They would value that, and along the way realise that God really was there, really did care, and really did answer prayers.

What follows is an imaginative reconstruction of a family giving such an offering in the time of Eli, just before the monarchy of Israel, about 3,000 years ago. The family has just heard that they are going to have a baby.

*There were fellowship offerings[13] to prepare, and so many people to tell. 'God has been so good to us, in giving us a child. We've got to share these blessings with our friends.' They rushed*

---

13 Leviticus chapters 3, 7, 19, 22.

*excitedly round to the neighbours. Indeed the whole village heard this news. The village grapevine was working overtime. 'God has blessed our family, and we are to have grandchildren. Our firstborn son is going to be a father at last. The Lord our God has kept us, and made his face smile upon us.' The words of the grandad-to-be were repeated dozens of times as he went round the village beaming excitedly.*

*'We must thank our God for this child to be.' So the family chose the very best and most valuable of the young bulls of the herd. It was an expensive gift; they were hoping to breed from this animal, and improve their stock. Still, God was worth this gift in thanks. They would take it to their local place of worship in Shiloh. There the ark of God still sat, symbolising the very presence of God himself. It was where the pillar of cloud used to stand back in the old days, when God had guided them so closely. It had been standing in Shiloh for some 300 years to date, as part of the Tabernacle of God set up through Moses all those years before.[14] The grandparents-to-be, with their friends around them, set off on the journey to Shiloh. They were fortunate to be living so close. Many would have had to travel all day to reach their local site to worship God. Living in Shechem of Ephraim, they were a mere ten miles away. They were also privileged to be close to Shiloh particularly, the main centre of worship for the whole twelve tribes of Israel. At the Temple, the family of Eli the great judge lived and worked as priests. True they did not think much of Hophni and Phineas, the greedy and selfish sons of Eli who worked as priests now, but it was still a privilege to come and worship here at this very special site. It was here where Joshua once stood, and parcelled out their inheritance from God, tribe by tribe. 'So sad that this modern generation of priests simply don't care about God the way that*

---

14 Psalm 78:60.

*we used to,' muttered Grandad as he contemplated the sad state of Israel these days.*

*Though they were only ten miles away, it was still a long and dangerous journey, down the valley from the Shechem pass, round the base of Mount Gerizim, and up the thickly wooded slopes to Shiloh. 'Ten miles used not to be so far,' grunted Grandad as they struggled up the final slopes to the Temple. He was relieved that once again their God had protected them from the robbers and bandits to be found in these hills in this lawless time, where everyone seemed to do whatever they liked, with no regard for God's laws, or justice.[15]*

*On approaching, they were relieved to find that Eli was still at the Temple, and would accept their offering to God. They really could not cope with the sheer greed of his sons. 'I wonder what God thinks about having such priests?' Grandad thought.*

*It was always awesome to approach God, and once again there was a hush as each of the members of the party came to prepare themselves to meet with God. They dared not approach even this close without thinking very carefully about God, praying, and reciting the great Shema:[16] 'Hear, O Israel: The LORD our God, the LORD is one' the grandad-to-be recited as his family approached the door of the Temple. Eli came forward, and greeted them warmly, remembering them from his earlier days of service as a family still really dedicated to the proper worship of Yahweh, unlike so many families these days.*

*'Welcome to the Tabernacle, the Lord's house at Shiloh,' Eli greeted his old friends (though many would not get such special attention, merely being allowed to enter quietly to pray).[17] 'You bring a sacrifice with you, I see. Let me examine it for*

---

15 Judges 21:25.
16 Deuteronomy 6:4.
17 1 Samuel 1:9–12.

*worthiness to Yahweh.' Though he knew that with this family there would be no attempt to cheat God, as so many were doing. As he did so, they told him the wonderful news about their family, and that God had at last granted them a grandchild to continue the family name. Eli gave thanks to God with them as he heard the wonderful news that here, once more, there would be a child brought up to honour the name of God, and that the glory of God would continue for another generation.*

*Inspection complete – this was indeed a worthy animal to give to God – Eli gestured them over to the altar of burnt offering, with them following rather cautiously. This was God's territory. God had obliterated people for coming here carelessly. Carefully Grandad passed over to Eli the unleavened bread cakes mixed with oil, and the wafers that were made without yeast and spread with oil, and also the special cakes of fine flour well-kneaded and also mixed with oil.[18] This was also to be part of the gift to God. Actually, it formed part of the priest's payment, as ordained by God, and Eli took it gratefully, knowing well the baking skills of this family, and looking forward to eating such delicacies as a gift from God's hand to him.*

*Bowl and knife in hand, Eli asked Grandad to place his hands on the animal's head, declaring it to be his gift to God in thanks for this wonderful blessing. Then, before anyone knew what was happening, there was one quick swipe of his knife across the bullock's throat, and the bowl filled quickly with the glistening blood, which was the life of this expensive gift that the family was bringing to God.*

*Eli took the bowl as the animal slumped to the ground, having given its all for the family. As he did so, he gestured the Temple servants to come and butcher the carcass for the sacri-*

---

18 Leviticus 7:12–14.

*fice. Then, in the part that always thrilled Grandad, Eli splashed the blood from the bowl around the base of the altar on all sides, a gift of a life to the great and fearsome God Yahweh, in praise for the life that he had given them. The gift was apparently accepted, as he was not struck down. God had once again agreed to listen to the thanks of his humble servant. What an honour! Then the servants returned, carrying with them a large bowl. In there were the young bull's kidneys, liver and fatty parts, all neatly washed, for Eli to offer to God. With a loud sizzle it was done. 'Thank you, Yahweh God, for your great gift to us, and your continued love to us, caring and watching over us year by year,' prayed Eli, and the family gave a heartfelt 'Amen. God is good.'*

*Then, with the carcass of the beast slung under a pole, they went off to roast the animal and celebrate together with the village over a great meat feast. There would be no shortage of food tonight. There was the roast beef, and also more of the fine cakes and breads from the same baking that had been offered to God earlier. The whole of the village joined in with the family, bringing their praises and celebrations to God for his goodness to this family.*

This was a tremendous time for the family to be together in the recognition of God's goodness. The children would learn a lot as they saw their parents and others publicly and sacrificially showing their love for the God who had done good things for them. It all happened so visually, it was not hard for the children to grasp the message of the events.

### (d) The sin and guilt offerings

(See Leviticus 5:1–19; 6:23–30; 7:1–10.) Both these offerings have the same basic pattern, but the guilt offering includes cases where saying sorry alone is not enough. Someone has been hurt, and that hurt has to be made better. The wrong has to be put right. There are several elements to this.

First, sin is serious, and cannot be lightly dismissed. Wrongs have to be paid for. Guilt exists, blame has to be attributed and the price has to be paid. In our society, blame is often laid elsewhere. 'It's not my fault' is a common cry in everything from the smallest family problem to major court cases. The idea of these offerings is that there is no escape from the fact that the deed was done, and a punishment has to be paid.

Second, it demonstrates the fact that the main person upset is actually God. He hurts when we do wrong things. God does see, and he cares what we do. This system certainly makes it costly to upset God. Adopting this set of values might well transform us, never mind our children. This set of values is certainly behind the New Testament when it gives that powerful teaching on temptation in James 1:13–15.

Third, we do have to say sorry to people as well. When we have hurt people, we need to put that right. This is costly, especially when we discover that merely paying for what the person has lost is not enough, but that they have to actually come out of it better off than they were before, at our expense!

## (e) Tithing

Israel, on top of all the particular sacrifices that had to be made, also had to tithe to God. A usual figure that is quoted is ten per cent, though that is merely a starting point (see Leviticus 27:30–32). The family's true sense of priority was demonstrated clearly. Children would see and appreciate that God meant so much to the family that the extra income that could have gone on toys, trips and ice creams was actually going to God.

## (f) Times of national praise or prayer

There were numerous occasions in Israel's history when the people gathered together for a special ceremony or rededication. In these times of special activity, the children also played their part; they were not ignored. They were part of the covenant community, and were therefore included. One of the great celebrations of Israel's history, the completion of the walls of Jerusalem (as an example), is described for us in two books, both times involving children:

> While Ezra was praying and confessing, weeping and throwing himself down before the house of God, a large crowd of Israelites – men, women and children – gathered around him. They too wept bitterly. (Ezra 10:1)

> And on that day they offered great sacrifices, rejoicing because God had given them great joy. The women and children also rejoiced. The sound of rejoicing in Jerusalem could be heard far away. (Nehemiah 12:43)

In times of national emergency, the children were also involved in praying, fasting, and calling out to God to spare them. There was no thought that the children were an unimportant part of the people of God, and therefore would not be needed on this day. The whole family came to call out. The prophet Joel said to Israel in a time of national need that they should all gather to fast and pray together: 'Gather the people, consecrate the assembly; bring together the elders, gather the children, those nursing at the breast' (Joel 2:16).

In a different time of national crisis the whole nation was summoned once again to seek God: 'All the men of Judah, with their wives and children and little ones, stood there before the LORD' (2 Chronicles 20:13).

*Summary*

There were many ways that a family was called upon to worship God; all of them were practical, and all of them could easily involve the children. A life that was lived for God in every department was a life that really spoke out to the children. It communicated the message that God was real, in a way that the children could not miss.

## 3. Weekly worship

'When the Sabbath came, he began to teach in the synagogue' (Mark 6:2). There was a weekly sabbath lasting from six o'clock on Friday evening (sun-down) to six o'clock on Saturday evening. Unfortunately, no information has survived as to how this was celebrated in early Israel. In later times it involved a visit to the synagogue, but before the synagogue was instituted we have very little information. We think that parents and children would have visited the local shrine. There they would have offered a sacrifice and the priest would have taught them.

*(a) The synagogue*

By the New Testament, and probably also significantly earlier, the weekly synagogue worship would have used the following pattern. The whole family would make their way to the synagogue, the adult males (including boys over eleven) sitting in one part and the women and children in another, to listen to the Shema: 'Hear, O Israel: The LORD our God, the LORD is one. Love the LORD your God with all your heart and with all your soul and with all your strength' (Deuteronomy 6:4). This was preceded by two benedictions and was followed in the morning meeting by one benediction and in the evening by two more. These were all recited at the lectern. Other prayers were also said: mostly praises to God repeated by one person with the congregation saying 'Amen'. Then the Pentateuch (the Law) was read, followed by a reading from the prophets. After a sermon or address the service was closed with a final benediction.[19] The family was expected to attend all of these services of worship. A child's interest in the things of God generally would be aroused and he would make more enquiries.[20] It is also important to note that families attended public worship together (see Deuteronomy 12:7 and Joel 2:16). In the centuries before synagogue worship, it is thought that there was less public reading, and more sacrifice in the service on the sabbath, but this is not really known.

Three pre-AD 70 synagogues have been excavated, and follow the same basic layout. This is quite helpful in showing us what the emphasis of the service was. The central floor had a public area built of stone for heavy wear and tear, with seats on all sides facing the centre. Rugs covered the very centre of the central floor, indicating that only a few people used it. The arrangement would allow free discussion among the congregation and let them hear speeches delivered from the centre of the hall and the lowest tier of seats. This placed the importance on the congregation, which assembled to worship, listen to the scriptural readings, and participate in instruction and prayer. There was no 'front' to elevate a person's status above others.[21] It was a people-centred place, about learning together, not entertainment, which sadly characterises some of our churches today. Presumably this means that there

---

19 J. A. Thompson, *Handbook of Life in Bible Times*, p. 347.
20 Eric Lane, *Special Children?*, p. 17.
21 E. P. Sanders, *Judaism Practice and Belief*, p. 200.

would have been fewer lengthy sermons, less of a performance mentality, and more change in variety of the people participating. While the subject matter could still be very heavy, this style would help children listening in with their mothers.

Synagogue services were not only for the sabbath though. They would also be held on feast days and in many places on market days as well. However, the synagogue was more than a centre for worship. It was a gathering place for friends, a school for boys, and the focus for local government. It was also a charitable foundation, as people in need were given gifts from the offerings made in the synagogue. As with church buildings, it was designed as the focal point of the community, not a strange building for a social group.

## (b) Sabbath worship

The sabbath itself was intended as a joyful time. It was a time to rejoice before God. The sabbath was not a fast, but a special feasting occasion. It is true that fires could not be lit on the sabbath itself, but food was left to cook or be kept warm on a fire lit before sunset on Friday. The Friday evening meal was as festive as people could afford to make it. The Pharisees devised special rules that allowed close neighbours to carry food and dishes from one house to another, and eating with friends or relatives was a regular event.[22]

Outside the synagogue, there was much to do in preparation for the sabbath. The family cleaned the whole house and then put on their best clothes, ready for sun-down on Friday. A meal was prepared beforehand, and candles lit. Then at sun-down no more work was to be done. A special day had begun.

No one who has been through a Christmas or birthday

---

22 *Ibid.*, p. 210

with young children can fail to realise the importance of this sense of a 'special day'. While the sabbath was held every week, its intention was to create that 'special' atmosphere that would make children feel happy about the day that they could spend together as a family worshipping the Almighty. Our society appears to have very negative feelings about Sundays as dull, tedious and empty times recovering from the wild excesses of the Saturday night, the purpose being to sleep for as long as possible, thus removing most of the day. Not so the sabbath as God intended. That day was supposed to be filled with God, not merely emptied of everything else.

The family spent the rest of the day between synagogue services as a family day, chatting, sharing, and just being together, which the busy weekday schedules would not allow. Towards the close of the sabbath, the family shared a final meal together, which was also full of symbolism, showing once more how central God was to their entire way of life. Comparing this to the way that we spend our Sundays (the Christian equivalent), there is often very little emphasis on God, or even family, over the whole 24-hour period.

*Summary*

In all of the worship that Israel offered to God, there was a place for the children. The worship was very visual and full of symbolism, all of which was explained by the family to the children from a very young age. The child was then encour-aged to participate in it and ask questions about it. The worship system of Israel had a strong emphasis on the chil-dren learning about God through seeing and doing. Incidentally, the combination of these two are seen in educa-tional circles today as being the most effective learning method.

## Conclusion

Israel taught their children about Yahweh as a way of life. God was essential to everything they did. The same should be true of people in the New Testament era. Education under the new covenant is very similar to that under the old. Christian parents are expected to teach their children the new covenant (gospel) as Israelite parents taught theirs the old covenant (Law). We teach them how to become children of God through Christ, and how to please Jesus who died for us, beginning with learning obedience to us as parents. Parents in the home are expected to do all this as it was in Israel.[23]

So God's prescriptive way to reach a child in the Old Testament remains true for our era today. The parents' teaching by example, and living a godly life daily, supported by the wider church family, is the clearest and simplest, the best, way of teaching children about God.

There are inevitably differences between ancient Israel and us, however; differences that arise from the change of covenant. Our children are not growing up to serve a godly nation but an ungodly world, in which they must find their way.[24] These differences make the work and experiences of our children more difficult. This only serves to highlight the importance of the family witness and lifestyle for the faith of an infant. This is because we need to give them the strongest possible foundation to cope with the pressures and difficulties that their faith will find in later years as they seek to serve their God themselves. It has probably never been harder to be a Christian in a state school than it is now, and to this we now turn.

23 Eric Lane, *Special Children?*, p. 41.
24 *Ibid.*

# *Part Three*
# THE PSYCHOLOGY
# OF CHILDREN

# 6

# *Understanding the Needs of Children*

Having seen how the Old Testament encouraged children toward faith, we will now look at modern psychologists' views on how children learn, and apply modern theory to the Old Testament approach. We will look at the Old Testament understanding of children and their levels of understanding first, and then modern Christian writers who comment on children's abilities from a psychological perspective.

## 1. The Old Testament

'Train a child in the way he should go, and when he is old he will not turn from it' (Proverbs 22:6). The Jews definitely had a sense of development in their educational structures, with specific ages at which it was appropriate to introduce new teaching materials. The Jewish fathers[1] described the following stages of a person's development.

Five-year-olds should be taught the Scriptures, beginning as we have seen with the book of Leviticus. At ten years the

---

1   J. A. Thompson, *Handbook of Life in Bible Times*.

children are ready for the Mishnah,[2] a more applied set of information. At thirteen years the children are ready for the Commandments, an abstract set of laws. At fifteen they should be taught the Talmud,[3] encapsulating complicated and abstract theological discussion and thought.

The Jews understood that children's capacity to learn and have faith develops over time, and their relationship to God needs looking at in different ways, depending on the stage of life they have reached. They had significant age markers for the development of their children, just as we have. In the previous chapters we have noted the significance of circumcision, weaning, the Bar Mitzvah, and the age of twenty. The Jews obviously had their own approach to the development of the child, and arranged their teaching programmes and relationships with them accordingly. As children have not changed in their need for psychological development, we still ask the same questions today. How do children come to believe, what intellectual changes do they go through on the route to adulthood, and how should our teaching methods take note of this?

For example, it is possible to consider the development in the faith of Samuel, from infancy to adulthood, by focusing on the way Samuel is described in the narrative of 1 Samuel:[4]

| | |
|---|---|
| 1:28 | Samuel is 'given to the LORD' for his whole life |
| 1:28 | Samuel 'worshipped the LORD' |
| 2:18–31 | Samuel 'ministered before the LORD' |
| 2:21 | Samuel 'grew up in the presence of the LORD' |
| 2:26 | Samuel 'continued to grow in stature and in |

---

2   Mishnah refers to a collection of oral teaching about the law of Moses which was passed on by rabbis.

3   The Talmud is a commentary on the Mishnah by later Jewish rabbis.

4   Gill Dallow, *Children's Ministry Magazine,* Issue 5, 1999.

favour with the LORD'
3:1–21     Samuel was 'called by God'
3:19–21     Samuel was 'constantly close to God'

Though there is no age clearly attributed to Samuel at any of these stages, he obviously began worshipping the Lord very early. Chapter 1:28 mentions him worshipping the Lord in the Temple when he had been given over to the priest for service. This took place, according to verse 24, 'after he was weaned'. Israelites were weaned late in comparison to modern society; but even so, this child is unlikely to have been much more than three or four years old.

In chapter 2:18 Samuel 'ministers' as a boy. The word is *na'ar*. We looked at the significance of this word previously: it usually relates to a youth, or pre-teenager, before maturity. Chapter 3, narrating the calling of Samuel as a prophet, begins in verse 1 with calling him a 'boy', and once again *na'ar* is the word used. So we can say that Samuel clearly began by being involved in the service of God as a toddler. Throughout his childhood he was regularly in the presence of God, serving and worshipping him, and helping others to do so as well. This continued until his calling by God as a prophet to speak before Eli, before he was even fourteen or fifteen. Admittedly he is a special example, being brought up in the Temple, and clearly under the hand of God, but the Bible only records such people. There are few records of children apart from these, so we cannot say how unusual it really was. All we can say is that God definitely can and does use very young children in his work.

In addition to the stages of life described by the Jewish fathers above, and what we see from Samuel's childhood, we can also learn about the practical outworking of these two models in the daily life of the community in public and family worship. This is visible in the festivals and family worship patterns that we looked at in Chapter 4. We have to accept that the Jews expected their children to be actively involved in a relationship with God from a very young age, and participate in the worship of that God along with the rest of their family members.

Another sense of progressive development comes from the use of objects in worship.[5] A child who can shake a *lulav* (palm branch) should understand what a *lulav* is for (worship of the saving God). A child who knows how to wrap himself in the *tallit* (prayer shawl) is obliged to observe the law of the *zizit* (threads on the corners of the *tallit*)[6] and pray properly and personally before God. So the boy's accepting of the responsibilities of the Torah[7] at thirteen was something that he had been building up to all his life. There is a process here, moving from the simple and visual, to the Torah, an abstract book of commands and lifestyles.

The Jews then clearly felt that children had a place in their worship, and that they should be encouraged in it in ways appropriate to their age. It was not only worship, however, but also confession that the Jews expected their children to be involved with. Children were regarded as being able to understand the guilt of Israel, share it and confess their sins.[8] Worship required an understanding of a glorious loving God, but confession of guilt needed a deeper understanding of a holy God and his commands, which should not be broken; and also of a method of forgiveness, should the commands be

---

5  W. A. Strange, *Children in the Early Church*, p. 17.

6  Tosefta, Hagigah 1.2.

7  The Law of God as seen in the first five books of the Bible, but specifically the Ten Commandments.

8  Gill Dallow, *Children's Ministry* magazine, Issue 6, p. 12.

broken. It seems that the Jews had a high view of the ability of children to understand God.

## 2. Modern writings

'We do, however, speak a message of wisdom among the mature, but not the wisdom of this age' (1 Corinthians 2:6). There are many modern theoretical models relating to the psychological development of the child. We will consider and compare several authors' theories of a child's psychological development in relation to the Jewish model. I have chosen those noted for their Christian stance, their general acceptance by the Christian community (as represented by the Christian nature of the publishing houses behind them), and the varied theoretical positions that they represent. In order to be able to compare them, however, we need to be able to use standardised terms for the stages of childhood and their capabilities. The first stage we will define as 'Emotional', the second 'Intellectual', and the third 'Volitional'. There are approximate age groups alongside them, but only with the comment that each child develops at their own pace. Some children will be a full stage further forward than their age might suggest, while others may be a full stage behind. The idea is to know your child's ability.

The first position we will examine, that of Francis Bridger, or James Fowler, identifies three aspects of faith – faith as believing, faith as trusting, and faith as doing. For this position, of these three dimensions of faith the second, trusting, is the key to relating saving faith to infants. The other two categories of believing and doing cannot apply as they need abilities which young children do not yet have.[9] So it is not

---

9   Francis Bridger, *Children Finding Faith*, p. 22.

really possible to speak of true faith in the earliest years of childhood, as there are intellectual abilities required even for the first levels of faith. In the earliest years, children can only believe, but they are short of real faith.

A second position, that of J. Westerhoff, has suggested four stages of faith rather than the three we considered above. These are experience, affiliation, searching and owned faith. Affiliative faith is where children merely join in with their surroundings and believe everything around them. The final stage of faith, 'owned faith', is the mature faith, practically an adult faith. This approach also holds out intellectual abilities required to achieve certain levels of faith, but it is happier to talk about real if limited faith at early years than the first approach seems to be.

The third position[10] we will consider does not have clearly defined stages that can be compared at all. There is not much sense of the idea that a child's faith can progress with their intellect, but that there is only a real faith adopted as and when God reveals himself.

Let us define the first two positions more closely, using our standardised framework:

*(a) Emotional: Stage 1* (from birth to six years old)

This relates to 'faith as believing' in the first position and 'experienced faith' in the second. We will consider for the moment the pre-school child, from birth to the age of their first two school years.

*(i) Pre-school days*   Here the only faith possible is that which the child draws from what they see about them. The

---

10 Eric Lane, *Special Children?*

child thanks God for his dinner, just as he is taught to thank his mummy and daddy. God is merely another member of the family; it is just that you can never quite see him. He has to be treated in the same way as the rest of the family. You have to talk to him, thank him, and say sorry when you have done things to upset him. In this case it is Mummy or Daddy that has to tell the child when they have made God happy or sad.

The child learns about this God through the family, through praying together, reading stories about him together, and worshipping God together as a family. Most of this will come through merely copying what the parents do. Children will not understand to any depth what all this entails, but can understand that God is real, and cares about them, and that they have to say sorry when they upset him.

We do need to sound a note of caution here, because at this stage a child will seek to please his parents and will naturally follow them whatever the example is. Therefore we have to say that the outward actions of the child do not necessarily reflect the enthusiasm and heart, and that the child might not really be saved. This is no more than saying that teenagers have the same problem, as do many adults. However, it is also possible that a child *could* be doing this from the heart. They *could* be seeking to love God, and say thank you, sorry and please to God as well as genuinely (or not) trying to do it to their parents. If they are genuine about this, that is all God requires. It is true that in an adult this response to God needs to be a lot clearer, and more carefully worked out, but at this age, such a response is all that a child is capable of, and it is sufficient.

Here the reliance of children upon the adults around them is the key factor. A child is emotionally dependent on the adults, and will follow the adults' lead in belief, if encouraged to do so. The most important factor at this stage of a child's life in creating trusting faith, therefore, is the child–parent relationship.[11]

What is particularly surprising is that there seems to be a possibility of faith from such a young age. In a previous chapter, we discussed the possibility that the child has not had the opportunity to do wrong at this age, and therefore does not really need salvation at all. We concluded there was little scriptural evidence for this.

If the child is to come to faith at this age, it will be faith in an invisible God friend: a further member of the family he trusts and talks to, and has to apologise to when he does wrong. It seems that the child can come to know this invisible God friend, whom his parents obey and follow, only through the pattern of trust in the parents. The theorists of the second position seem happy to accept that this includes even very young children from birth to thirteen months.

According to this position, our problem with this would be due to our sense of expectation that faith has to be expressed in adult terms that a child of such a young age is incapable of.[12] This leads to a sense of incredulity among adults, and a belittling of the child's faith experience, and cynicism when hearing of child conversions. Such a response ensures that nobody takes the child's faith seriously, and nobody nurtures the child, with the result that the child's spiritual life dies for lack of support. If this happened in the physical realm, there would be public outrage at such neglect, but because it is in the spiritual realm such shocking neglect goes unnoticed.

Another danger that this pressure for an adult-style commitment produces is that it asks for a wholly inappropriate response from this age group. It encourages them to

---

11 Francis Bridger, *Children Finding Faith,* p. 29.
12 *Ibid.,* pp. 35–36.

parrot abstract ideas that they cannot grasp, merely to make the adult happy. This may do considerable damage to their chance of discovering faith, as it acts as an inoculation, shielding them from really considering true faith because they think that they already have it since they can make certain statements that please adults – even though they actually mean nothing to them. An example of this happening might be when a child affirms belief in the virgin birth. This is a good evangelically orthodox statement, and suggests that the child is progressing well in her professed faith. However, on further questioning, it is apparent the child thinks 'virgin' means that they don't eat meat (confused with vegetarian). The child has no problem with the correct labels, but has no real idea of what they mean, and so her use of them could not point to a true faith.

The Jews had no difficulties with this. There were real activities and expressions of faith that the children were expected to understand and be capable of enjoying with God. These activities and expressions were relevant to their personal level of development, and they allowed the children to express their faith in a way that was meaningful to them. Children would have been encouraged in those beliefs by their whole family, and especially their parents, ever since birth.

*(ii) School days*   The second part of this stage comes when the child goes to school for the first time. One of our theories includes a break here, and adds a second stage, 'affiliative faith' (infant and junior school age, from four to eleven).

The real reason for defining this as a separate stage is the development of social abilities within the child. For a pre-school infant, the world consists almost entirely of the family, and friends of that family. This stage is marked by major life changes such as going to school or nursery. All of a sudden there are a host of other people, other world-views and ideas, other ways of behaving, and other people who want attention. Life does not consist entirely of the family way of doing things, and it is a shock for the child to suddenly discover alternative points of view. This is not usually revolutionary at first, because a child's set of values and their understanding and ability limits what they come into contact with. The children may well make some penetrating comments, but those will be based on brutal honesty and innocence rather than a grasp of complex and abstract things.

Yet, as the child grows, particularly into junior-hood, opinions form, and become stronger. Then, what their friends think about something is equally valid, if not more important, than what Mummy and Daddy think (especially if Mummy and Daddy have been a bit vague and inconsistent about their beliefs). Putting an age on this level of development is difficult, for some reach this very early, while some never move beyond this stage. Here faith is kept, made or broken, often simply because their friends think that way too.

A sign that the child has started to reach this stage is questioning the existence of Father Christmas. Parents will sigh now, for they know that this signals the end of a trusting childhood, and that the horrors of adolescence are just around the corner.

A child that demonstrated an emotional faith has to overcome the hurdle of discovering that their friends do not know anything about this God, and do not believe in him. A real faith can overcome this, but there are many that lose any appearance of faith now. The parents and their church leaders need to be particularly clear, consistent and encouraging at this point for the child. When all the values in the world are being wobbled, the child needs to know that the parents, or church leaders, really do trust and know God. They need to know that all the things they have seen and been told are still true, despite what others say. They need to know that their faith is real, works, and is placed in a real God. Here the Jews had a distinct advantage in that there was no major culture shock in matters of faith or upbringing for the child in this stage to undergo. All the children they mixed with would have been children of the covenant, and should have been brought up in the same way. Problems in Jewish society reflected the unfaithfulness of the parents rather than the system.

*Summary*  Trusting with instinctive feelings and mimicking the behaviour of those around them is the foremost feature of faith in infancy.

### (b) Intellectual: Stage 2 (Junior: 7–11 years)

This is linked to the 'trusting' stage of the first model. The second model's 'searching' stage begins towards the end of this period, pushing on slightly into the third stage we will identify below.

As children grow and develop, they become more able to reason. It is at this sort of age that things like Father Christmas and the tooth fairy are discovered to be untrue. For many children, the stories about Jesus can also suffer the same fate, unless they see that the stories are based on something more truthful than the stories they also learned about the tooth fairy. They need to know 'why'. Actually they really only need to know that the parent understands 'why'. If they do, then all is well. At this stage, the parent's faith (or that of the spiritual role model, whoever that is) has to be genuine and visible, in order that the child does not abandon faith in Jesus along with faith in Father Christmas. The rapid growth in the ability to absorb knowledge at this age means that the intellectual component of faith becomes much more important.[13]

If the child has grown up with faith from infancy, then this element of trusting is likely to continue in this period. Now, however, more searching 'why' questions will be asked, and lives that support the teaching will be necessary. The patterns of covenantal trust established in infancy continue to provide the emotional framework for faith in this time of rethinking of his faith.[14]

This stage is a good time to reach out to the unchurched child. It is a time of natural curiosity that extends to religion, especially if the child meets believing children their own age. Here, if this is the first contact with religion, it will be 'what' rather than 'why' which is really asked, although this age of child seems attracted to the question 'why'. For example, before this stage, children would accept the fact that Jesus died on the cross. Now they will want to know 'why'. Really they want to understand, but not in terms of atonement theology, merely that a friend takes the punishment for another because he loves him so much. Practical knowledge, not theoretical, is the key here. Children can come to a simple understanding of Christian truths here, such as salvation, sin, and response, providing the teaching is done in a simple, practical way full of illustration. In the teaching of children of this age, though, the information has to be specific and literal. That is how children think. Any discussion of the fact that 'God is everywhere' over breakfast is likely to result in serious concentration, followed by the question 'Does that mean he is in the jam pot too?' Doing

---

13 Francis Bridger, *Children Finding Faith,* p.45.
14 *Ibid.,* p.50.

is bound up with being at this stage.[15]

Children are a lot nearer to the Old Testament way of thinking than you or I will be, with our abstract intellectual faith. At this stage, then, faith is believing because it seems likely, but mainly still because someone they know and trust clearly believes it, and lives as if it is true in practice. There is a growing intellectual content to faith. A faith that began in the previous stage is now growing and developing reasons for its belief, drawn mainly from people they trust.

*(c) Volitional: Stage 3* (secondary education, from eleven up into maturity)

This marks the period of adolescence, and relates to the 'doing' stage of the first model. The second model identifies this as the third stage called 'searching faith' (secondary school age, from eleven upwards). By this stage children have developed an ability to reason more logically and abstractly. They are able to make logical reasoned decisions independently of adults and peers around them. It is a time for choices and for the formation of an adult personality. It is the beginning of a capability for true abstract thought.

This sort of response tends to happen in teenage years or later (or indeed never in some people, though occasionally earlier also), where the individual considers 'why'. This is the time for seriously questioning everything, and testing all the values they have ever held. In school at this stage, they are being exposed to a wider world-view and learning new ways of examining everything. A choice of the will here is likely to remain throughout their adult lives.

Abstract concepts are therefore teachable at this level, but as always they should be backed up by lifestyle. Here the child

---

15 *Ibid.*, p.52.

will be examining their faith more carefully from a logical point of view. Abstract ideas have to be worked through now, and the child may worry over apparently illogical things. The Trinity or the omnipresence of God[16] for instance might be a major difficulty for some at this time. For others it might be creation or evolution. They do not need university-level answers, but they do need to know that other Christians have faced this, and worked through it before them, and that there *is* a light at the end of the tunnel. That needs communication, and a trusting, talking relationship. Unfortunately this stage also regularly happens during the teenage years, where this very relationship is often strained to breaking point. Such a relationship has to have been built up over the previous years with open sharing and conversation about God together. Any difficulties with this relationship, and the chance to witness to the teenager may well be strained to a point where the teenager rebels altogether.

There is a faith to search out and discover. It is an important stage to go through, for out of it arise the more carefully made statements of trust and belief that we are more used to accepting in churches. We cannot make our declaration of faith in the 'atoning sacrifice of the incarnation of the omniscient Son of God' until we have done some serious searching for ourselves (if not taken a Bible college course)!

Children can make stands on principles here. A child may decide to stop stealing, or swearing, or choose not to fight any more, and a host of other things that will set them apart in the playground as different. They have deliberately decided to follow Jesus' teaching. While capable of the abstract, their faith must still be grounded in reality, and in practical things. Training for them at this stage must include a consideration

---

16 God being everywhere.

of the abstract questions, but there must also still be a heavy emphasis on the practical. The abstract must still be applicable to school life.

The Jews also understood that the child now needed more serious instruction, and started teaching the Commandments at this stage. These are abstract, but all have a very logical base. The chapters following the Ten Commandments in Exodus 20 are full of expanded explanations of real-life scenarios, as if to answer the very questions of this age group.

However, perhaps the more important element for the child at this stage is that of the group. What are their friends doing? Standing alone is very difficult for people of any age, but especially so at this tender impressionable stage. This has been called 'affiliative faith'[17] for this reason. It is where the child accepts the standards of their chosen peer group. They place faith, commitment, and trust in their peer group. The fact is that teenagers will identify with what their friends accept rather than find an individually thought-out faith.[18]

This leads to a serious problem with backsliding, or the losing of faith, among people of this developmental stage. Identifying with one group, they can apparently show real faith, then as they lose touch with the one group, and move into another circle of friends, they behave in another way, and demonstrate an apparent loss of faith. This is a well-known phenomenon especially among youth clubs. We have to be prepared to watch teenagers apparently move in and out of faith at this time, as their allegiance switches back and forth.[19] This developmental model explains psychologically why it is that so many of our youth show promise, then disappear. It

17 J. Westerhoff, *Will Our Children Have Faith?* (Seabury Press, 1976).
18 Francis Bridger, *Children Finding Faith*, p.67.
19 *Ibid.*, p.70.

leaves us with the question over their faith, however. Was their affiliative faith real and saving? (This discussion moves us off into a different direction, and is beyond the scope of this book.)

Again there are many that lose their faith at this stage, being persuaded by other world-views and systems. The faith of their peer group might no longer seem relevant or sensible, perhaps even babyish. Genuineness, and an ability to talk openly and frankly with young people out of a long relationship of doing so, will be the most important thing here. If God has always been real to them, then faith as a teenager will not be a problem, but could prove an exciting time. If he has not, then it is quite likely that they will become another one of the many teenage casualties lost from church youth clubs today. This is again a problem encountered more often in our society than it was in the ancient Israelite one. There the older person was the place to turn to for practical wisdom, and the father or mother particularly. Today old age and parenthood are often things that are despised and rejected. The Old Testament teenager had role models older than themselves to turn to, and expected to be able to do that in a way that is rarely possible today.

There is an interesting example of a father who had lost this respect and authority from his sons. Genesis 19:14 tells the story of Lot, who was in a city about to be destroyed by God. God had given him advanced warning of this, and Lot was running round gathering his family to rescue them. However, his life had simply not backed up this message, and his sons-in-law simply thought he was joking. There was no basis of relationship there to talk about God. Lot, it seems, had never done so before, and so the sons-in-law did not think much of him going all 'religious' now. They thought it was a wind up! It would be funny, except firstly it often happens in homes today, and secondly, Lot's failures led to the death of those sons under the wrath of God.

*(d) Owned faith: Stage 4* (from puberty into adulthood, at whatever age the child becomes an adult)

This is still the 'volitional' stage for the purposes of this chapter. Finally the long search is over; the person is intellectually able to be convinced of the claims of Christ and is able to give himself over meaningfully to following Christ as an act of will. Here we speak not so much of children as mature adults, who have their values set and world-view established. It is not likely that there will be any other major changes in their opinions about things from this time forward. What they believe now, in essence, they will believe for the rest of their lives, with minor modifications rather than wholesale changes in direction. If a person has made it this far, it is likely that their faith will remain with them in some form through the rest of their lives. Obviously this is a gross generalisation, but, being that, it is generally the case. The child is mature, and has made a 'choice' in life. This is what we often consider that we should be looking for in 'a decision'. Through bitter experience we have come to be suspicious of claims to salvation from all ages, until they have reached this point. However, such a stage is moving into adulthood, and therefore beyond the scope of the book. Additionally, I believe that this stage is clearly reachable before adulthood, and we can speak of a real, 'volitional' faith long before this, providing the support and trust relationships are properly in place.

## 3. An alternative model

This is the third model that we briefly introduced previously.

Here there is no attempt to identify the specific stages of the other positions separately; this model considers them to be more of a gradual process than a series of milestones.

### (a) Conversion is a process not a crisis

A child growing up in a Christian environment will be exposed to a Christian way of life, not just words. Jesus will become a familiar name to them and will be seen as an important member of the family. Family prayer times at bedtimes and mealtimes, for example, will become a way of life, as will regular church services and activities, including clubs, weekends away and so on. All this will become familiar, a way of life, instead of a strange, novel and confusing environment. This will affect the child's moral, emotional and spiritual development, and train the child to a life of living with God naturally. This is the way of the Old Testament, and it is a gradual process. The Bible says:

> Fix these words of mine in your hearts and minds . . . Teach them to your children, talking about them when you sit at home and when you walk along the road, when you lie down and when you get up. (Deuteronomy 11:18-19)

In support of this approach, there are many Christians whose experience of the gospel has not been one of crisis and conversion, but one where they cannot remember not believing in God. Their conversion was a slow gradual process. For them we must still speak of conversion, but it will have been in an environment of growth rather than crisis. If we speak of conversion we must do so in gradual terms of change. This does not mean that no change took place, rather that it happened slowly, at a time when thinking had not hardened; when habits were unformed and the character was undeveloped. The experience was not one of change so much as growth.[20]

### (b) Conversion is not decision, but growth

In terms of the covenant benefits which we considered in an earlier chapter, children brought up to accept the existence of God, and hearing the stories of what God has done, have an in-built advantage, as the Old Testament child did. Yet whatever this position suggests, there still has to be a conscious decision for themselves that their sin has upset God, and that they have to ask God to forgive them. Then they can enjoy God as their special friend. The child is capable of making this decision at a very early age, and therefore becomes unaware of this decision in later adult life, merely aware of the consequences of it that are ongoing.

### (c) Children have a natural faith

Another belief in this model of child salvation is that children have a natural faith, which works to the advantage of the evangelist. They take the world at face value and accept what is told them. If they are told that Jesus loves them, and that God exists, then that is fine. However, they are also told of the tooth fairy and Father Christmas, and happily believe in them too. We need to be aware of the dangers here, and make sure that our presentation of Jesus to them is more real and vital than the fairy tales they are told.

However, the natural faith of a child is not the same thing as saving faith. There has to be a difference. It is true that children are more likely to take things on trust than adults and this really helps the work of encouraging them to adopt a saving faith. Yet their trustfulness does not in itself mean a

---

20 Eric Lane, *Special Children?*, p. 71.

saving faith. If the words and ideas the child hears include God, sin, and Jesus Christ, he will slowly become capable of responding in an expected way to these labels. He will be able to believe that God is there, although unseen. He will have difficulty in understanding how this can be, but don't we all?

It is not until children gradually come to see that naughtiness and disobedience constitute something serious in the eyes of this unseen God who is there, that a real use of the word 'faith' can be used. If at the same time (if not earlier) the stories and acts of Jesus are introduced, it will become possible to relate Jesus both to God and our sin. At that time the child is able to respond to God and understand the way of salvation and deciding whether he wants it personally.[21]

*Summary*

This model is prepared to accept conversion of children from a very young age, though there are several cautions. We must be very careful in boldly proclaiming the conversion of a child (or anyone of any age) until there are real fruits demonstrating that conversion. That is especially true of children who are prone to believe in whatever an adult they trust tells them. Yet it is equally true of any adult conversion.

The stages of development for this model are not as important as the reality of the conversion. Nevertheless, in the model there is an awareness of the child's development from emotional, through into the intellectual before a third stage ('volitional') is reached. Conversion therefore can be defined as 'real' from all three stages, but its outworking is that of a process rather than a crisis alone.

---

21 *Ibid.*, p. 82.

## Conclusions from the three psychological viewpoints

The first two models are essentially similar, although the second model separates the 'emotional' faith into two stages. What is noticeable is that both start the process of 'possibly having faith' very young indeed. The second model also moves the 'volitional' beyond adolescence and calls it 'owned faith'. Other than that, the two are effectively the same.

So from these models, 'faith' needs to be associated with the child potentially from the beginning of his life, at least as soon as he can respond to the parent. The parental role of teaching the child about God, as well as about life, begins at the same time. That time is from birth, in order to encourage the right habits, which reflect the standards of God.

At the other end of the process, the second model pushes genuine, lasting, owned faith into an adult environment. This removes something of the problem of backsliding so common among teenage groups, for their faith is still under construction, and may well change significantly yet, along with all the child's other values. That is a useful distinction in terms of explaining the high rate of loss among young people to the church, but it has difficulties also with the definition of what 'faith' really is.

The difficulty is that it implies that the earlier stages of faith are not real faith at all, merely 'phases' through which a developing child is passing. How many parents confront young converts with the remark: 'It's just a phase, you'll grow out of it'? The dismissal of real faith at this point can have a damaging effect on children, who know when they are not being taken seriously, and they can easily resent it.

Adding the third model into the process highlights the need not to be too rigid about these age groups. Children mature at very different rates, some smoothly and easily, others violently, with massive swings in personality and responsiveness. Some of this is due to environment; some is due to the child's personality. It is here that Christian parents need to avoid being too harsh on themselves. When one child turns peacefully into a teenager, and another becomes a little monster overnight (and it can happen that fast), the tendency is to assume that one set of parents is better than the other set. This can be a very false picture indeed.

At whatever rate the change, a child very clearly goes through certain stages in development, which are linked to changes in the society the child lives in, and the ability and personality of the child. At each of these stages we can talk of the possibility of genuine salvation for the child from a very early age. From the moment of salvation onwards, there will be a lot of pressures and changes brought to bear on the child to challenge that conversion, perhaps even more than an adult would have to face. They also face those pressures with far less spiritual support usually than an adult would have.

Another warning that modern psychology would give us is that children are vulnerable and trusting. It is very easy to force a child into making a form of commitment that later proves not to be genuine. Faith at whatever age needs to be tested and to bear fruit. This is not to say that faith in children is not real, any more than it is to say faith in adults is not real. It needs to be tested and to bear fruit in all ages before we can be encouraged about its genuineness. It should also make us cautious in the way the gospel is presented to children, especially children of non-Christian backgrounds.

This presents no difficulty when compared to the Old Testament viewpoint on a child's spiritual development. Both consider that faith is a developing thing among children, and there are definite stages within a child's ability to respond to God. Both also accept that children can hold real meaningful faith from a very young age indeed. These stages, then, need to be adopted into our understanding of children, and they need to affect our strategies for winning them, and nurturing them within the family of God.

# 7

## *What Is the Moment of Conversion?*

The statements in the conclusion of the last chapter really need to be challenged from a theological rather than psychological perspective. Are children really saved, and if so, at what point? When is a person truly converted? What marks that moment?

Here we are treading in difficult areas, for the only one who can ever know when a person is truly converted is God himself. So if this discussion is to be practical rather than abstractly theological, we can only work in areas of vague generalities. We can only talk about people that behave as though they are saved, and give us every reason to think that they are saved, showing what looks like the fruit of salvation (Galatians 5:22). Before this can be discussed, though, there are some theological assumptions that have to be made. I believe that once a person is truly saved, they belong to God's family, and cannot lose their salvation. It may be that they live lives away from God as backslidden Christians, but they are, all the same, really saved, and really going to heaven. Once the gift of forgiveness is given, it is not taken back by God. On the other side, it is also true that many will appear to be saved, using the right words, for reasons of their own, but never actually are saved. Only God really knows people's hearts.

The reason for spelling this out is because we have already noted that there is a genuine problem of children apparently losing salvation. This phenomenon is something we saw in the psychologists' models. The first two models both appear to talk happily of infants becoming Christians, and then losing their faith. I maintain that the Bible teaches this to be impossible. Either the infant still is a believer, though not living like one, or their profession of faith was only to please the adult originally (a real danger in children's work), and not genuine faith at all. The reason for this is at least two-fold.

First, in a discussion of child salvation, there is the enormous problem of children saying they believe in God one day, and then saying they don't the next (perhaps slightly exaggerated). This is often due to peer pressure, and loyalty. It brings into question the genuineness of the conversion, as well as the genuineness of the present attitudes the child shows.

Second, the church's attitude to children can be to blame here, not really thinking that the child's salvation counts for anything until it is an adult one. This leads to a lack of follow-up and after-care for the young Christian, which often leads to the person struggling and apparently losing faith. For a definition of salvation we need look no further than *Thank You, Jesus* (Children Worldwide, p. 11). This was the booklet used for children's counselling in the Mission England campaign with Billy Graham in 1984, and thus represents mainstream thinking on the subject:

1.  I must believe that Jesus died and came back to life.
2.  I consider myself one of God's family. I am prepared to

love and obey Jesus, though I understand that being a Christian will sometimes be difficult.

## 1. The Jewish approach to child salvation

'On the eighth day they came to circumcise the child' (Luke 1:59). In the Old Testament, the genuineness of conversion would not have been a question at all. The priest would have asked if the boy were circumcised. If the answer was 'yes' then he would treat him as a child of the covenant. He would assume the child to be a believer until the child demonstrated otherwise. It was all part of being in God's covenant. If the answer was 'no', the father would not come before the priest anyway, but the child would be treated as an unbeliever by the community until he demonstrated otherwise. As a baby the child was dedicated to God through circumcision, and the community made its promises to nurture the young child, and teach them about God. The child would grow up in an environment where they would be expected to meet with God, pray to God, and follow through all the daily and yearly rituals with their family. This was simply because God was every bit as real as the rest of the family were. There is never any debate in the Old Testament about when to evangelise a child at all. It would never have occurred to them to do so. They merely emphasised the constant need for them to obey and honour their parents. This included honouring Yahweh the God of their parents, which had to be done through a practical hands-on daily living out of a relationship with Yahweh, as well as it did with their parents. This was a down to earth approach designed to encourage the child to faith. This is opposed to our more modern style of allowing children to develop as they please, and then imposing faith from outside at a later date, on top of already existing values. The idea was 'Train a child in the way he should go, and when he is old he will not turn from it' (Proverbs 22:6).

The child was encouraged to accept the family's set of behaviour patterns based on the idea of a covenant relationship with God. It was not necessary to understand these in adult terms. The child's behaviour in relation to God related to the appropriate stage of the child's understanding. Some children naturally rebelled against this and were disciplined by being put out of the people of God, removed from the synagogue, or even stoned (Deuteronomy 21:18–21). Nevertheless, the children were encouraged to try God's way first.

Applying this attitude to the modern church, then, the children of believers, who have been baptised or dedicated as infants (depending on which church tradition you come from), ought to be treated as believers too (until they demonstrate otherwise), by both the parents and the church. This is not due to covenant theology. It is due to the child's exposure to God through the family, from birth. This is designed to encourage their response to him, in the same way as (and as soon as) they respond to their parents. They should be coming to faith naturally, as they learn to feed themselves, or learn to walk. We are all aware of people who are unable to put a date on their conversion experience, who can point to no specific time or conscious decision. This is because, for them, it appears to have been a gradual thing, or that they have 'always' felt that way. For them, following Jesus became a way of life (in admittedly a very basic sense) from when they were too young to remember. There is no reason to suggest that such a conversion is 'unreal'.

Sadly, the lifestyle of modern families in society, and the thinking of the church, tends to mean that the child learns alternative ways of living and thinking first. Then as a youth or perhaps at Sunday school he hears the leaders try to introduce a belief in God from outside his experience, despite having Christian parents. The child is assumed to be a pagan rather than a saint, and is treated as such. Train up a child as a pagan, and do not be surprised at the result. He will be much harder to evangelise.

## 2. Salvation in the new covenant

'And this is my covenant with them when I take away their sins' (Romans 11:27). It is obvious to say that the New Testament is built on the Old. It is a mere extension to say that the New Testament idea of salvation is therefore based on the Old. What we need to ask is, 'Have there been any changes in the New Testament that affect this understanding?'

Salvation in both Testaments can be defined as the point when a person of any age learns to trust in God for themselves, genuinely saying sorry for what they have done wrong, and wanting to please God from that moment on, and receiving God's forgiveness. This is in line with (if phrased differently from) the definition given above. Taking that definition means that there are no changes between the Testaments. People today are saved the same way that they have always been: by faith in the work of the Messiah, the Christ (either looking forward to it, or back upon it).

What *has* changed is the emphasis. In the Old Testament there was a big emphasis on family, and corporate lifestyle, with the assumption that all in the family were inevitably believers. The children had to follow the ways of their parents, and learn to love God for themselves. With the conquest of Alexander the Great 300 years before Christ, came the Greek world and Greek thought. This contained the idea that we should be coldly logical, individualistic, stoic, and able to identify cause and effect in everything. This had an impact on Jewish and then Christian thinkers and theologians studying the nature of faith.

Over the next few centuries, into the early years of the church age, the faith of the individual became an affair of the intellect, not of family experience – Greek not Hebrew thinking. The effects of this way of thinking are not really there in the New Testament itself, where there are several examples of children of believers being baptised along with their parents at the time of the parents' conversion. This follows the Old Testament concept of family faith. However, Greek ways of thinking became more obvious in the writings of the early church fathers, and the developing theology of faith.

## 3. Salvation in the church age

'For it is by grace you have been saved, through faith' (Ephesians 2:8). In the intervening centuries, from the early church fathers to the present day, this change due to Greek thinking has led to an emphasis on the idea of a personal salvation for everyone by the preaching of the gospel. It has taken us away from an idea where a believer's children will naturally learn to love God for themselves by 'breathing it in' from their family. There is suspicion cast upon a person who cannot give a time and an experience to their conversion, but merely attributes it to their very early childhood.

There has to be a decision process now, because that is the way the Greeks expected to see things, within the rules of cause and effect. The Hebrew world operated on community and warmth, the Greek one on logic and thought. Our society is still based very much on the Greek way of thinking. That has, as we have said, led us to suspect 'conversions' based on relationships in childhood before the child is capable of logical argument, and only to give value to a decision based on logic. That is not a biblical approach, but a cultural one.

Spurgeon in his 1864 sermon 'Children brought to Christ not the font' worried about the church's attitude to child conversions when he said:

> My brethren you have no more right to suspect the sincerity of the young than to mistrust the grey-headed; you ought to receive them with the same open-breasted confidence with which you receive others when they profess to have found the Saviour.[1]

The church often still follows this Greek pattern, waiting for children to make decisions of their own, on a rational and logical basis[2] rather than respond emotionally to the God of their parents with the same trust given to those parents. It is a shame, because there are many adults even who respond to God out of emotion and identification rather than logic. We must remain free from insisting on a logical intellectual approach. We come to God with our love, trust, and emotion far more often than we do with cold logical deduction. Therefore there is no reason why a child cannot respond in faith to God. They are perfectly capable of these things, providing we do not insist on complex knowledge or response beyond the capabilities of that child.[3] Children are better equipped to come to God with the Old Testament saints, responding to the love and care of God they feel, trusting blindly for the future, than they are with the gospel presentation approach which appeals to the intellect.

---

1  Eric Lane, *Special Children?*, p. 84.
2  Which, as we have seen, is not usually intellectually possible until they are teenagers.
3  Penny Frank, *Children and Evangelism* (Marshall Pickering, 1992), p. 20.

It would be very unfair of us to expect children to be able to give us complicated theological explanations which are beyond their mental capacity. God is able to meet with them providing they can understand very simple concepts about right and wrong.

## 4. Salvation among children of non-Christians

'What advantage, then, is there in being a Jew, or what value is there in circumcision?' (Romans 3:1).

### (a) Juniors and above

There is no discussion in the Old Testament about children of unbelievers coming to faith, for the Jews were not very strong on evangelism. Jonah was not at all impressed when God asked him to become an evangelist (see the whole book of Jonah). Yet this is an area of interest for us. From what age can children who do not have this direct and pervasive teaching about God actually understand and be genuinely converted?

What we can say from the Old Testament about proselytes and God-fearers is that when they joined the Jewish faith they had to be aware of several things:

1. They had to be able to say that there was only one God, Israel's God, and that he was real.
2. They had to submit themselves to the laws of God, in worship and sacrifice. They had to attend the Temple, or Tabernacle worship, and later on the synagogue worship.
3. Proselytes also had to become circumcised as full members of the covenant community. It was also possible, as we have already discussed in an earlier chapter, to remain a God-fearer, and not become circumcised.

There are many more requirements in terms of observing the Law that we could consider, but they would be on a personal or adult basis. For instance, proselytes (when adult) also had to pay the tithes that were due as full members of the Jewish community.

Looking at the three criteria listed above, there is nothing that a junior school child cannot understand and accept themselves. This is providing they have had them carefully and practically explained, and even more carefully demonstrated by the evangelist. The evangelist will become the role model for the child in the usual place of the parents, and will have to live out this teaching for the child to copy. In spiritual terms, the evangelist becomes the parent for the child, starting to fulfil the role of the parents from the first section above.

A child who has not been brought up to believe in Jesus may attend a mission or club in which the Christian faith clearly makes sense to the people who run it. The child likes and trusts these people, and this gives a sense of truth and trustworthiness to the things that they teach. As a result the child may often decide to incorporate some of the leader's beliefs into his own life. Time alone will tell whether these come to occupy the dominant place in his way of thinking but it is possible in principle that they will, even prior to adolescence.[4]

It is therefore possible to evangelise unchurched junior school children successfully, but not in the same intensive way as we might a believer's child. Evangelism in this case means becoming a role model living out the gospel. The evangelist must gain the respect of the child, and encourage the child to live in the way that they do. Paul after all did this when he

---

4   Francis Bridger, *Children Finding Faith,* p. 123.

asked others to imitate him, as he imitated Christ
(1 Corinthians 11:1). It then begins the process that the
believer's child is privileged to have from birth. It begins it
with many disadvantages, having only limited access to this
lifestyle, and having already developed an attitude to religion
from parents, and peers, which is probably not helpful. The
child might have unlearning to do before they can make
progress toward God.

*(b) Infants*

Could an unchurched child meaningfully make any commitment before junior school age, when they are able to
think and grasp only simple concepts and world-views?
The answer here again appears to be yes; providing the
evangelist can demonstrate to the child by their lives powerfully enough that God is real. Obviously, the younger a child
is, the fewer people are really influential in the development
of the child. Before infant school age, it is really only the
parents, regular childminders and very close family that can
have any input at all. Evangelising a child of three needs a
good and lengthy contact with the child in order for them to
see God in the evangelist. Such contact is unlikely, but
theoretically possible. So, while it should be technically
possible for an infant of unbelieving parents to learn enough
to be saved, it seems unlikely that there will be many
opportunities for it.

## 5. Are child conversions false?

'Many will say to me on that day, "Lord, Lord, did we not
prophesy in your name?"' (Matthew 7:22). There is a problem
in child evangelism in that many children who tell their
parents that they love Jesus as very young children, will often

fall away later in life (often quite quickly). I accept that in many cases this is because the child did not know what they were saying. In many cases, it is far easier for the child to say something merely because they think that the adult wants to hear it, especially if it is their parent doing the asking. This means that really the child is not responding to the God shown by the parent, but to the parents themselves.

How can we avoid this difficulty? We need to employ a gentle and gradual approach. We should never push for conversions at any given moment, but in fact do all we can to encourage them to delay, and count the cost. Encouraging them to put the decision off may ensure a more genuine conversion experience when the child does insist on it.

Some would suggest that 'coming to faith' does not have to be a sudden, decisive, one-off act at all, and this entire debate is unnecessary. We do not need to interrogate them with questions like 'Have you done it yet?' Coming to Jesus is not an 'it' like washing your face, cleaning your teeth, or making your bed. It is a journey or a developing attitude. The children may keep coming, finding out more. The first occasion may get lost in the mists of time. There is nothing wrong with considering four or five such 'conversions' in a child's life.[5] One reason why children apparently become Christians, and then later on abandon their faith, may be due to this over-pressuring of our children (admittedly from the best of motives and a real urgency to get them 'saved').

While there is some truth in this idea, it is still important to maintain the biblical concept of a moment, a rebirth, a particular time of repentance and changing loyalty, even though for some this may be indefinable. Biblical doctrine teaches it, and we should insist upon it, while recognising that

---

5 Eric Lane, *Special Children?*, p. 92.

the experience of some means that they cannot actually pinpoint the precise moment.

This means that we should not apply pressure for conversions, but should be willing to ask children to 'wait', and we should teach sanctification on each subsequent time that a child comes to 'make a decision'.

However, I am convinced that the real conversion of a child can be very early, and among Christian parents who are living their lives in the way that God intended, it should be so. The child should absorb the knowledge of God and the love of God from the parents. The family home should be so clearly showing that God is real, cares, and loves that child, that there should not really be a matter of doubt in the child's mind. There should merely be a taught obedience to God, along with the taught obedience to the parents. Such behaviour on the part of the child, who can understand nothing more, is just the same as the behaviour of the Old Testament saints who knew nothing more. Perhaps later there will be rededications to God as the child grows and reassesses what they mean by 'being a Christian' in their changing and developing world. These can look like 'conversions', but would be better labelled as 'rededications'.

In fact, among the children of Christians, it seems that 'child evangelism' should not be necessary at all, any more than it was among the Jews. The real focus of this should be with the children of unsaved parents.

## 6. The children who give up Christianity

'No one who puts his hand to the plough and looks back is fit for service in the kingdom of God' (Luke 9:62). In our modern secular society, children are being confronted with many different ideas, arguments, and world-views. It is no surprise that children from junior school age upward find it difficult and confusing to cope with Christianity. Even being taught Christianity in schools today, the children also have to compare it with other religions described as equal to Christianity. Christianity in schools is at best merely 'one way' of many. It is no wonder that the faith of today can be over-turned and become the non-faith of tomorrow, all depending on the crowd that the child chooses to 'hang out with'.

With such pressures and belief-swings, can there be biblical saving faith that transforms lives and is effective for eternity? Again, it is hard to generalise. A child acting in this way might be genuinely saved, but a backslider for a time. This happens among adults, and we acknowledge it; it also happens among children. We have seen that the church rarely gives children enough encouragement to keep their faith and grow in it. Any children that do become Christians will often be poorly fed spiritually, and encouraged to live the life of an adult Christian that is meaningless to them. This is because (as we have already said) the church often regards their conversion with too much caution, and does not follow them up as carefully as they would an adult convert.

Parents and churches do not know how to teach and encourage the faith of little children, because they often do not really understand the nature of that faith, or the level of children's understanding. There is little follow-up or attention given to the children who do profess to have become Christians. In an age where follow-up is well recognised as essential to the growth and establishment of a true and lasting faith among adults, it is surprising to see how little effort there is for children in this area. Perhaps most damagingly of all, the Christian parents themselves do not really demon-strate God in the home as clearly as they should.

If we lose many children who claim faith, is it their fault?

Were they never saved? Is child evangelism therefore an irrelevance that bears false fruit? Alternatively, is it really our fault more often than not for only doing half the job?

## 7. If a child can be saved, what can we expect, and when?

'The children of your servants will live in your presence' (Psalm 102:28).

### (a) Infants

When teaching an infant about God, we might major on the idea of God as a loving parent. The child would relate to God much as he might to a parent who is not in the room at the moment. They know God is real, and that God can be made happy and sad, just like their mummy and daddy can be. God is just a bigger parent. Not a grandparent who has a totally different relationship usually, but a bigger parent, whom the child's parents have to obey and follow too. The child at this age knows that they have to say 'sorry' to God when Mummy and Daddy tell them that they have upset God. This is the same as when Mummy tells them they have upset Daddy (or vice versa). The Old Testament lifestyle encouraged this.

So, in summary, children can say 'thank you', 'sorry', and 'please' to their physical parents, and accept that along with their parents, they can also say 'thank you', 'sorry', and 'please' to God as well, who is real even though he cannot be seen. Children can also know how to obey the simple rules of the household, which are God's rules over them, and also over their mummy and daddy. They might think, 'If Mummy and Daddy do it with me, then it must be right and I will talk to and obey this God I cannot see, along with my parents.' It is an adopted faith, but real as far as it goes.

## (b) Juniors

For a junior school child, we would expect to see faith in concrete terms: an assertion that 'God is real' or that 'God answers my prayers'. The child will ideally be praying, with the parents, and also alone. They should be joining in the church services, in worship and prayer (in ways that are meaningful to them). They are also capable of reading and understanding Bible stories, and discussing them and their relevance. They should be doing this at home, with parents who also accept the relevance for their own lives, and openly share with the child what the story must mean to them. They should also get this discussion at church, in the Sunday school, as well as midweek clubs. Ideally there will be a Christian Union at school for them as well, which would give them more support.

At school, the child will be able to tell other children about God, and be able to live out their faith in the playground. Here, not stealing, forgiving others when they are nasty, receiving bullying sometimes without striking back, and many other very practical things, will be important. The child will have a lot to do in living up to their faith. Here the parents (or role model evangelist) must really help them, following up the child's conversion properly, and helping the child to deal with the difficulties. Again the Old Testament lifestyle encouraged this, when it gave the child a role in worship that was practical, visual and exciting, but above all constantly explained and lived out among them.

## (c) Further developments

As the child grows up, and understands more, there may well be a further response in the heart of the child to the gospel. This could resemble that of initial conversion, and may even be more dramatic. However, if the initial experience was real, this is not a true conversion at this point, but would be better labelled as a rededication. The Jews focused on this a lot with their ceremony of Bar Mitzvah, a rededication of the young boy to God. By secondary school age, conceptual thinking has started, and the child will be capable of understanding and participating far more. Abstract thoughts will be easier, and the child can start to join in the discussions with the above groups on a deeper level. They will be able to take in more of the sermons as well, especially if aided by worksheets from the preacher, giving the main points, perhaps with questions and pictures along the way to help them keep in touch. In Jewish thought the child was now almost adult, and could take public part in the services along with the other adults, in reading in public, or praying. Encouraging the faith of children in this way in public worship becomes very valuable.

## Conclusion

It is my firm belief that children of Christian parents ought to be receiving all the teaching they need from their parents (although I admit I am one who has failed in this respect). The church and any other organisations have only got a supporting and secondary role. Parents should encourage their children to have a real faith in God from as early an age as they can have faith in their parents. It will not be a very complex faith, and will need a lot of refining over the years, but it is capable of being a real one. Providing the parents both take that faith seriously and nurture it, the child should not backslide from it.

Children of non-Christian parents will be more reachable once the child draws their influences more from outside the family. This will usually be at junior school age. There it is certainly possible to reach them, and for them to have a real and saving faith. It will, however, require an investment of time and love in their lives, as the evangelist earns their trust and becomes a role model for them.

This conclusion is controversial, because conversion is often defined as an intellectual process, which excludes children because of their inability to think in abstract ways. However, we must always avoid the danger of insisting that God works in the same way in everybody, and believing that unless the convert can use adult terms, they are not yet really saved. We know that children are incapable of that. Children are merely isolated from adult understanding by intellectual development. Can not the living God still communicate and save despite these limitations?

*What should I do about it?*

Below are some main points arising from our discussions, which you may want to consider and act upon.

(i) We have to state along with the Bible that true conversion is profound, life-changing and lasting, at whatever age it happens.

(ii) We have to allow from our bitter experience that some will fall away, however old they are at apparent 'conversion'.

(iii) We have to accept our responsibility to follow up the new convert, and encourage them to live a prayerful obedient life to God, showing them how it is done, and from where to get their help.

(iv) We have to assert that God is not limited in the ways that he deals with people in bringing them to conversion. He is capable of saving children of whatever age as well as adults of whatever intellectual capacity.

(v) We have to admit that the church generally is not really geared up to reaching children in the way that appears most effective. We try to reach them as mini-adults, which they are not. This means a reassessment of our outreach policy to children as a church, and our parenting policy at home.

(vi) As parents, children's workers, and also churches, we have to reassess our policy of involving children who are Christians. They need to know that they have a valued and relevant place in the family at worship, as well as the church at worship.

# 8

## A Survey of a Family

This chapter is in the form of a questionnaire filled in by a particular family in order to see if the principles and theories developed in previous chapters can actually work in the modern society we live in. It is my firm belief that if any principles and theories developed here are unworkable in our society, even though they may be in line with the Old Testament and modern theories, then they are useless. I have chosen this particular family because they have been trying to put these principles into practice for some years, with mixed success.

In order to protect their anonymity, the individuals are assigned totally fictional names, merely as the first main characters in the Bible relevant to their sex. The age of the children is close to their actual ages in order to preserve the significance of their answers. The family consists of a father (Dad), a mother (Mum), two lower-end secondary school children – a son (Adam), and a daughter (Eve) – and a son (Abel) of nursery school age. The approximate ages are given in order show their level of understanding in relation to their age. Abel did not complete the questionnaire, as some of the

203

questions were difficult for him to understand. The parents are both involved in full-time Christian work, with a special focus on children.

## The survey

'Follow my example, as I follow the example of Christ' (1 Corinthians 11:1). If you dare, it might be helpful for you also to answer these questions as a family.

*1. Who is responsible for teaching children about God?*

DAD:    In order of priority, the father carries the main responsibility, then the mother, then the church.

MUM:    Dad is responsible, but Mum does more of the actual contact time.

ADAM:   Mum and Dad / holiday clubs / Spring Harvest / church.

EVE:    Mum and Dad / holiday clubs / church.

ABEL:   Adam and Eve.

*2. How do you think children should learn about God?*

DAD:    At home, as well as through the local church, and Christian events like Spring Harvest. Through being taught Bible stories as a foundation, and Bible principles being applied in the home. Through experiencing God in everyday situations with the guidance of parents. Through being taught through the church, and by experiencing God within the body of the church.

MUM:    By life experience. They need to see it being lived, to learn to read the Bible, and understand it from experiences, by talking to God for themselves, and seeing God answer them, and learn from the church group as well.

ADAM: By going to youth groups, going to church and reading the Bible.

EVE: By being with other people at church and youth group etc. and being told about God. It is good to read the Bible regularly too.

## 3. How have you tried to implement this?

DAD: I try to teach by modelling the life that I want my children to live in my own life. Spending time with each of the children reading the Bible, and stories. Including them in the work that my wife and I do among children. Encouraging children to go to Christian clubs for systematic teaching and training. Involving them when they want to be at Christian events with us. Teaching the children Bible stories and scriptural principles, then trying to apply these to things that happen day by day. For instance, how should we react to bullying, being short of money, being ill, having crabby neighbours, etc?

MUM: By living it out together. For example, we pray about stuff together, and read and apply the lessons from the Bible together. The family is a member of the church, and we belong to a community of other believers, and we learn from the Bible there as well.

ADAM: By a steady and calm process.

EVE: By doing the things in my previous answer.

## 4. Has it worked?

DAD: I am happy to call Adam and Eve Christians and they live it out in a way that has been demonstrated. Yet the weakest point in our family faith is not having enough quality time as a family together. It is a gradual process, so ask me if it has worked after we are all dead. Seriously, training works better than just teaching. Our kids usually know the right thing to do, but like us they do not always do it!

MUM: Yes, Adam and Eve have their own personal faith. Abel is talking about praying . . . saying 'sorry' for naughty things he's done.

ADAM: Yes it has.

EVE: Yes.

## 5. Does it help your family life together?

DAD: Yes, it is at the centre of what we are.

MUM: Yes, in teaching and strengthening together, moulding each other.

ADAM: Part of Dad's job.

EVE: Yes.

## 6. At what age did your children become Christians, and how?

DAD: Adam and Eve became Christians when they were very young – I can't put my finger on exactly when. They grew into a relationship with God, then one day wanted to say 'sorry' and accept God's forgiveness. It was probably when they were four or five. They both asked for baptism at about ten or eleven. Abel has a relationship with God which is particularly expressed in his bedtime prayers. He knows that we love Jesus as a family, and doesn't question his existence.

MUM: With Adam and Eve it was gradual, obvious in both by about nine, and they were baptised at ten and eleven. Abel became a Christian very recently.

ADAM: About five.

EVE: The age of four, by Mum and Dad reading Bible

stories, singing songs and telling us of what God /
Jesus did for us.

*7. Have you seen any signs of God dealing with your children at
a very young age?*

DAD:    Yes, they have always wanted to go to meetings,
which is not normal without God's Spirit, I think.
They both felt the voice of conscience, especially
Adam. Eve has often had pictures and ideas she
feels come from God. They are both keen to witness
to their friends. Abel responds to being prayed for,
especially if he is upset or frightened.

MUM:    For Eve and Adam, God speaks to them when they
have 'run-ins' with us, with each other, or with
friends. They never miss a thing of God's dealings
with them.

ADAM:    I cannot remember any specific way in which God
dealt with me at a young age.

EVE:    Yes.

*8. How have your children developed in their relationship with
God as they have grown?*

DAD:    Gradually. They started from a point of unques-
tioning belief, moving into more questioning belief
and a more complex relationship.

MUM:    Since camp (at the age of nine) Eve has grown in
confidence and never questioned or really wrestled
with it since. Adam is steadier, he just prays. Abel
has understood more and more.

ADAM:    I have become more interactive at church. I am
listening better to the preaching. I have been going
to meetings where we pray for revival all evening on
my own, and enjoying them.

EVE:     I have developed in God by going to church,
         Christian camps, being with Christian friends and
         learning and reading parts of the Bible.

*9. Do you think worshipping God together as a family is
important?*

DAD:     Yes, but if it is forced it can have a negative effect. I
         think it is particularly valuable to provide space for
         households to spend time in family groups in
         church-based all-age worship to get families used to
         worshipping together. We have not been very
         successful in having set mealtime devotions, though
         we have tried. They become monotonous now the
         kids are older, but we do still always give thanks
         before food.
MUM:     Yes.
ADAM:    Yes.
EVE:     Yes.

*10. How do you treat Sundays as a family?*

DAD:     They are different in that I do not do regular office
         work. If we are not working (i.e. taking part in
         services) we spend the time recreationally or
         relaxing. At times, because it is our work place, if we
         are not working we do not go to church at all,
         particularly if Mum's parents are with us, unless
         they want to come. We try to treat it as a day to
         relax, and to spend time with God.
MUM:     Not in the way I would like to. Sunday is a work day
         rather than doing fun things together, which I
         would prefer.
ADAM:    Church, home or park – unless with Grandma and
         Grandpa. On my birthday we missed church and

went bowling.

EVE: We go to church whenever we can, and try to focus on God more.

## 11. Do you read the Bible together as a family?

DAD: Yes, but rather intermittently.

MUM: We tried to read it after breakfast, but since our hours of leaving in the mornings are so different this is no longer happening. We have tried teatime reading but feel that just reading isn't working any more. Kids want reading and possibly discussion. The different ages of the children makes this difficult.

ADAM: Normally . . . after tea, sometimes.

EVE: Yes.

## 12. If so, how do you do it?

DAD: We have used various Bible storybooks at breakfast time, but we now have breakfast at different times.

MUM: Answered above.

ADAM: Dad reads, and we talk together.

EVE: Usually after tea at the dinner table – we take it in turns to read parts.

## 13. Do you pray together as a family?

DAD: Yes, but not in a very clear pattern.

MUM: Yes, about issues as they arise, e.g. lack of money, trouble at school, illness etc.

ADAM: Night / morning / over a meal. Normally, sometimes on my own.

EVE: Yes.

ABEL: At bedtime . . . with Mummy and Daddy.

*14. If so, how do you do it?*

DAD:      We pray with each child individually at bedtime, and highlight things important to our family and church. We give thanks for God's love and provision. We give thanks at mealtimes, and often draw in other subjects, as they become important. I feel that we do not read or pray together enough.

MUM:      As above! As things happen, we try to pray together whenever there is a need, or whenever God has answered a specific prayer. We have not settled on any real set time except often at mealtimes. We do give thanks and pray for a particular person if a newsletter has come in from them.

ADAM:     With my parents. On my own. In different places / in trouble / for people with particular needs.

EVE:      We used to have a prayer board with photos of people that need prayer and take it in turns to pray for a person.

*15. How does your local church approach children, and families in worship, and does it help you?*

DAD:      In our church, children are taken very seriously and their faith at whatever age is treated with great respect. We have just baptised a seven-year-old who has shown real evidence of living a Christian life, and has made a clear commitment to Jesus.

          Yes, this helps us because our children know they are a valuable part of the church. We have never had to drag them to a meeting, and we have to ration their attendance mid-week. They are encouraged to take part with their own worship practice once a month, and many kids bring their own instruments, flags etc. to meetings. The kids' groups are modelled on training the children rather than just teaching them.

MUM: The church has a positive approach to children and wants to provide a good environment for them to grow in their relationship with God. Sometimes the worship really is helpful, but sometimes it is not. It all depends on who is leading a lot of the time.

ADAM: The church thinks kids are important. They have an all-age service. They also have kids' music practice. We play drums and sing bouncy songs.

EVE: Our church has a family service every month, a toddlers' group, and infants' group, a juniors' group, and a youth group . . . yes.

ABEL: Yes, because we dance and sing, and play musical instruments. We have Sunday school.

*16. Are there things that you would like the church to do, or arrange, that would help your family to worship God?*

DAD: More regular training and encouraging courses for parents would help people develop parenting skills, and communicate the church's expectation for how children should behave, and get involved in the life of the church. More specialised training to help children develop special skills would help – healing, training, speaking, etc. These already happen, but need to be more regular. A children's house group would also be of great benefit, but we do not have the staff.

MUM: More worship opportunities outside the church building, linked with practical things like evangelism and fun.

ADAM:    More services that children are running.
EVE:     No.

*17. Can you describe the pattern of regular events that would happen in a standard week? This is to get a feel of the balance of things in the week.*

DAD AND MUM:

Sunday          Interactive all-age services twice a month.
                Kids' group once/twice a month, separate from adults.
                All together with children from other congregations once per month.

Monday          Prayer meeting – often for sick people.

Tuesday         Prayer for Revival meetings – children are encouraged to attend – or cell groups in homes.

Wednesday       Club for 5–7s.

Thursday        Mums and Toddlers.
                Coffee bar 10.00–2.00.
                Club for 7–11s followed by club for 12–14s.
                Different cell groups in homes.

Friday          Monthly kids' worship practice.
                Often an Alpha group (day time).
                Youth group.

Saturday        Monthly there is a social event in someone's home, organised by a mum, for 10–11s.
                Occasional kids' clubs outings – bowling or skating etc.
                Servant evangelism sometimes, like gardening and car-washing for people in the neighbourhood.
                Occasional training events.

ADAM:

| | |
|---|---|
| Monday | A special club twice a year. |
| Tuesday | Revival meeting. |
| Saturday | Servant evangelism, like car-washing, for people in the community. |
| Sunday | The church service. |

EVE:

| | |
|---|---|
| Sunday | Church service in morning, youth congregation in evening. |
| Monday | Prayer meeting (maybe). |
| Wednesday | Cell groups in church members' houses. Infants' club. |
| Thursday | Junior group. |
| Friday | Healing meeting. |

*18. What sort of discipline do you use in the family, and do you make a distinction between house rules, and God's rules?*

DAD:  I think we are quite strict in terms of discipline. Having lived in third world countries (and boarding schools) our kids are not allowed to leave food, and have been trained to eat whatever is put in front of them. We try to make a distinction between childish irresponsibility, which needs correcting rather than punishment, and deliberate defiance, which needs to be punished. We both believe that smacking has a part to play, but alongside other discipline tools, and we try to encourage, commend, and reward our children regularly. We try to say 'sorry' to them when we are wrong.

We do not make a distinction between house rules and God's rules, as house rules become God's rules in as much as the children are expected to 'honour their mother and father' in the rules that they make.

We do, however, try to teach our children what the Bible says about issues that relate to what they are and are not allowed to do.

MUM:     We try to give clear boundaries of behaviour and explain the consequences of being disobedient. There is a strong emphasis on trust, truth, and honesty. We want our rules to be like God's rules, based on the Bible. As the children grow older there is more negotiation possible on some of the rules. Some will always remain, but we are trying to instil some sense of responsibility as they get older. This requires more freedom and trust, which doesn't always work, so when it doesn't we have to withdraw a little freedom until they are ready. With Abel it is a little more straightforward as he is younger and there is less room for freedom in his own decisions. When we are thinking of right and wrong we will talk about godly behaviour, asking them if they feel their behaviour is good, and promoting the good of others before themselves.

ADAM:    Quite fair discipline, and quite well linked to God's rules.

EVE:     Mum and Dad make the house rules to try and make sure we all get on with each other and are brought up well. God says we must obey our parents, so it is important that we obey God's rules and the house rules.

## Conclusions from the results of this survey

Some very interesting parallels can be drawn between the Old Testament approach to family life and the life of this family. Being a modern family, however, there are also difficulties where the modern society life rubs awkwardly with the Old Testament pattern. These are worth looking at.

## Conclusions from Question 1

*Issues about the leadership of the family*   The whole family feels that the father is the head of the house, and is therefore primarily responsible for the spiritual development of the child, as he is also for their physical and emotional needs. This is certainly in line with the Old Testament, but may be a little unusual in modern society. However, the mother appears to feel that although the father is the head, she does more of the actual hands-on work with the children. This is probably because she is around with the children more often than the father is.

The children feel that the parents are jointly responsible for looking after them, and meeting their needs, but recognise that they also get a lot of their teaching and direction from the church and special events like Spring Harvest. This is also in line with what we saw in the Old Testament, with the father taking the main responsibility. The mother perhaps has more practical dealings with the children, certainly in the early years. The wider family, in this case the church, local and national, also has input with the children.

Sadly this is the reverse of the pattern that we often see, where the local church is given the main responsibility, and the family assumes no responsibility at all. The mother might have some spiritual contact with the children, but the father rarely has contact at all. As a nation, our attitude to parental responsibility for the spiritual development of our children needs a lot of rethinking.

This family also suffers a common problem of modern society: the father is away from the children a lot. His type of employment means that he has many more chances to be with his children and influence their development than most fathers do; but it is still a difficulty.

Interestingly, the youngest child has learned a lot from the older children, and considers them to have been the main spiritual input in his life. This too would reflect what happened in the Old Testament community. There the older children (especially the firstborn) were the role models for the youngsters.

### Conclusions from Questions 2, 3, 4 and 5

*Issues about where the children learn about God*   The family feel that their home is the main place for learning about God, and that it is done mainly through involving God in the everyday events, and encouraging the children to involve God in those everyday events. This is the 'training rather than teaching' method the father mentioned. The mother, who is again the main contact for the children spiritually, particularly expresses this in her answers, though the whole family mirrors it. This same principle of involvement with God is carried on beyond the home into their church life, and beyond into the wider church at special meetings and major events. God is seen as involved in everything the family does. He is part of the life of the family, not something boring to deal with on Sundays or special occasions.

Again this is what the Old Testament suggested, where the home was the main place where the children learned from the parents that God was involved in everyday life. This lesson would be reinforced locally as they gathered together weekly on the Sabbath, and then nationally as the great festivals came and went. The pattern of living out faith in the home, reinforced locally in church, and then nationally, has worked both in this family, and in the Old Testament. What God outlined then still works today.

The parents see their faith in God as integral to the life of the family. The children seem to assume that this is just the way it is. Mum and Dad are like that. This suggests that involving God in their lifestyle is natural to them, not strange or unusual. Such an attitude is (from my experience) rare and very commendable.

From the answers given, and my own knowledge of the family, it is clear that the children are individually responding to God, and their lives are changing in the light of the practical nurturing they receive from living in this sort of environment.

### Conclusion from Questions 6, 7 and 8

*Issues about the reality of children's faith*   The experience of this family appears to demonstrate that children can become Christians at a very young age, and maintain that witness through school years, given the right teaching and encouragement. The parents, interestingly, give a later date for conversion than the two older children themselves do. In fact, the father was not clear in his answer about the youngest child's conversion at all. Perhaps this reflects the innate caution of the parents in only accepting the conversion as genuine when there has been some growth and fruit for that faith. This is different for their youngest child, who has (according to the mother) recently become a Christian.

The father was questioned further about this issue and replied with the following:

'In response to the question of when our children were converted, I would say that it is almost impossible to identify a specific point at which they came to Christ. All of them developed a relationship with God that first became evident when they were about three, and they began talking to him in prayer times, and asking us questions about him. Eve had a period of doubt around the age of eight, but was deeply affected by camp when she was nine, and has not shown any sign of doubt since. Adam has had a steadily growing understanding of God, and a deepening prayer relationship, which we have observed. Both asked for baptism, and went through a baptismal class with an elder in the church. They wanted to make a public declaration of faith.

'I do not doubt that children can receive Christ at a very young age – about three, I think. Conversion is not a very helpful word in the case of our children, though, because we have not observed them convert from one kind of life to another. Rather they have gradually developed a relationship with God, and somewhere – maybe imperceptibly to us – there has been a point where they have been born again.

'Abel certainly seemed to receive revelation from God when he grasped the fact that we need to be sorry for the things we have done wrong, and ask Jesus to forgive us. He understands that Jesus died on the cross to take our punishment, and says that makes him feel sad. He has said 'sorry' to Jesus. I am not 100 per cent sure that he is born again – because I am not God – but I am 100 per cent sure that he has a relationship with a God he believes in undoubtingly.

'I feel that all three of our children felt that they belonged to the family of God before they came to a moment of actually saying a prayer of commitment.'

From the experience of these children at least, it seems true to say that the nature of the children's relationship with God fits with the understanding we examined earlier. It is limited to what the person is capable of understanding. Over time, the children have developed, and are now able to express their faith in more developed statements and beliefs than previously. Naturally, there are also times when they are more obedient to God than others. As they learn obedience to their parents, and society, they are also learning obedience to God. Nevertheless, there is real evidence of a true work of God in the hearts of these children.

The faith of these children has been tested over time and has borne fruit in witnessing, and withstanding persecution at school. The parents have provided some of this information, but I have also observed the children over some years, and the way they express their faith personally. The older ones have also had times of doubt, and come through them with a stronger faith. The children have shown a sustained desire for God, wanting to go to meetings and learn about him. They have also had experiences of God speaking to them and supplying their needs. The older ones are certainly aware of times where God has clearly acted in answer to prayer. Even the youngest responds to being prayed for and draws encouragement from it. According to the mother, the youngest (nursery school age), though very young, has recently made a profession of faith.

The parents have expected their children to respond and grow with God, giving them the time, trust and acceptance that their faith required to develop. Many parents wait for the children to become teenagers before really expecting any serious spiritual responses, or before giving any serious spiritual input.

### Conclusions from Question 9, 11, 12, 13 and 14

*Issues about family devotions*   The family recognise that their family life is very busy, and that it is difficult to set aside particular times to worship God together. They have been having difficulty, with their daily timetable, to establish anything regular and organised. Things have been tried over the years and have worked for a while, but it is difficult to maintain a regular pattern. Also, as the family has grown up, the needs of family devotions have also changed, and what worked once no longer does. Reading the Bible together as a family is a difficult task to do meaningfully over a prolonged period, and there isn't a simple 'answer' that will solve their problems in this area. It needs constant monitoring and changing.

However, it seems to be more important to live out the truth on a daily basis in practical things, trying to integrate God into all areas of the family, than to give formal teaching on a regular basis. That way, the teaching is more practical than theoretical. This has certainly been true of this family.

I have known of other families where the Christian life was lived out in a forced and legalistic way, and it became counter-productive. The children switched off and in teenage years came to resent the time spent in this way and resisted the teaching that the parents gave. While we must show caution in defining cause and effect so directly in this way, the way a family approaches their Christian life in the home has to be very important too. Perhaps what is most significant from this study is that teaching about God has to be incorporated into the family life on a general level, reinforced by the whole family trying to obey all of God's commands. It is probably more important to show your children that you are *trying* to obey God and have a regular time together, than it is to succeed regularly. Allowing the children to see the parents struggling in trying to be obedient to God is itself an important lesson for children to learn.

Praying together is also important and difficult to keep as a regular pattern and event. It needs to be constantly worked at. This family tend to pray over issues as they arise. They have a prayer board with photos of people needing prayer, and other things to stimulate the attention of the children. They are encouraged to pray for needs and situations both within and beyond the family. Then they will see God's answers more clearly. This is an area where modern families tend to fail, for they tend not to look to God for practical everyday things where they can see answers directly. They do not often actively involve God in their daily lives, and therefore the children never learn that God really does care and meet every need.

For this family, bedtimes are important for family prayer, as are mealtimes, but they are even more vital when there is something important to discuss with the children. Praying for the current needs of the family together is vital, because it helps them to confirm their trust in God along with their parents. This was the great strength of the Old Testament system, when God was to be relied upon for everything, from the rain, to the sun, to crops growing, to animals being safe, and to the family being protected along the way. There was an ordained family pattern in which the whole family would take part regularly, at least once per week on the sabbath, but usually at many other times through the week as well. Here perhaps the family surveyed (along with most other families including my own) are not staying as close to the Old Testament pattern as they might.

*Conclusions from Question 10*

Sunday can be difficult, and it is important that the children do not feel they take second place to 'going to church'. However, it is also essential that they understand that worshipping God and keeping the sabbath for God is also important. Time has to be given to the children, especially in this society when parents are often not with their children during the daytime or even early evenings in the regular

school week. The family we are considering does this sometimes by not going to church at all on certain occasions. This
is to remind the children that time spent with the family is
very important, and that the children as individuals are also
important to the parents. This family's answer may have
surprised you, but may actually be quite wise. However, on
most occasions, the family all go to church together, because
this is where God has called us to meet with other believers,
and to worship him. This family are unusual in that their
work revolves around Sundays, so it is their main workday.

This is not the usual attitude towards church attendance,
where many people hold going to a meeting as almost sacro-
sanct. Many seem to think that the number of meetings they
go to can determine their spiritual state (I write this comment
as a minister who has also counted heads on Sundays and
worried when so and so is not there). Clearly this is not really
true, and can end in damaging people's faith by overpressure
on their lifestyle. Having said all this, of course, if the family
rarely went, or often did not bother going, that would send a
different message. It would warn the church that something
was wrong, and would also tell the children that God was not
really worth bothering with. The answer, as in so many things,
has to be a balance.

The Old Testament rarely talks of meetings, other than the
main annual festivals. It is the modern church that has placed
an over-emphasis on meetings, to the detriment of honouring
God among families in the busy society in which we now live.

## Conclusions from Question 15

The church makes the children feel welcome. This probably
helps the children want to go to church and accept the
message of the church as being for them. This is a very difficult balance to achieve and maintain for a church. The

children are clearly an important part of the congregation
and need to feel valued and involved. Yet they are not the
only group in the church with particular needs, and many
going to that service might feel ostracised or unwelcome
because of the emphasis on children. Balancing the needs of
the different people groups in the congregation is extremely
difficult.

The particular congregation in mind here has a strong
orientation towards family and children in some of its
services, and has separated off the older youth congregation
completely on occasions, so they can worship God in the
rather more noisy and energetic style that they prefer. All
branches of the church come together for a celebration service
regularly. This suits this particular congregation. To follow
this one church as a perfect pattern, or one with the 'answers',
is clearly wrong. Each leadership must seek to fit the needs of
its congregation in a way most appropriate to its own situation. Different stances in theology, personality, demographics,
and socio-economic grouping, to name a few influences, will
all affect the decisions that a church must make. What
matters is that these issues have been thought through.

The Old Testament patterns of worship were also varied,
with their times of solemn holy quiet, as well as their times of
noisy party-style rejoicing. Indeed, different times of Israel's
history provided different styles of worship. For instance, the
worship in the wilderness during the time of Moses was
rather more formal and organised than it would have been
during the time of the Judges. At that time, worship was
much freer, and less structured. Consider, for instance, the
sort of worship system implied by Micah's behaviour in
employing a personal priest in his home in Judges 17:10–13.

Each congregation and each time period has to find the
styles of worship which most adequately allow the entire

congregation (including old and young, unemployed and employed, male and female, and any other interest group) a valid part to play. That was clearly the original purpose of the format of worship God gave in the beginning. Children are definitely part of the congregation of God and should be included in the services.

## Conclusions from Question 16

Whatever is being done, more can be considered. More can be done to develop children's faith and spirituality better, to train children for future leadership. Better training for the parents is important. Another thing is to expect more from the children. This will encourage the children to deliver more. This is something that every teacher knows from experience. If you expect little from a class, or a child, then you receive little. Children need to be encouraged, stretched and pushed a bit. If this is true in secular education it is equally true in spiritual development. The parents and churches of our children need to take this idea on board, and create challenging opportunities.

Beyond that, as children mature spiritually, they need to have roles appropriate to their maturity. In adults this translates into leadership functions and responsibility. It should do the same with children in ways appropriate to their physical age and mental maturity. The church and family should seek to provide more leadership roles for maturing children, and more nurturing and training for children, suitable to their abilities.

The Old Testament society pushed hard, and brought children to maturity far earlier than our society does. While we may feel that our society is better, in that it allows children to have a longer childhood in terms of general responsibility and labour, we do our children no favours by making them stay in *spiritual* childhood beyond the time when they can develop.

In fact, by holding them back, we are in danger of stifling their development, and discouraging their enthusiasm.

## Conclusions from Question 18

There is no distinction between God's rules and family rules in this family's answer. This is very important for children, because consistency and fairness are crucial, and God's rules and character are fundamentally based around consistency and fairness, though 'justice' is the word applied more commonly to God. Family rules in the Old Testament were God's rules anyway. They are ideally suited for family life. After all, God designed the family.

Of course, individual applications of God's rules will be developed as the children grow up. Thus the rule that Mum and Dad should be obeyed when they issue a ban on a five-year-old from crossing the street will need to be reinterpreted in the case of a fifteen-year-old.

Once the children accept the standard of God's rules within a family, then they are more willing to accept the concepts of sin and punishment as well as that of forgiveness, which again seems to have been borne out in the lives of these children.

## Overall conclusions

The principles and practices that we considered from the Old Testament, have been carried out quite well in this family.

As in the faith of the Old Testament, they are trying to live out their faith in their own family life, and involve the children in praying for the needs and difficulties of the family. The children are encouraged to have a real and natural faith in the God who, while not visible, is the head of their house. The father takes the lead role in the home, and the family as one follow him as he follows their God.

Outside the home, this approach is being supported in the local church, as a wider family for the children. Beyond that, there are national level meetings where once again the children are receiving the same message.

The message to the children throughout is that *they personally* are valued and important to God, to their family, and to the wider family of the church. As such, they are encouraged to express their faith in God personally, and publicly.

The family does not do so well in areas where the modern lifestyle clashes with the Old Testament one. This is primarily in the following areas:

1.  *Time.* The family finds it difficult to make a regular time where God's word can be discussed in a meaningful and realistic way together. Modern life is considerably more crammed with different responsibilities than Old Testament life was.

2.  *Discussion.* The family finds it difficult to adopt a pattern of discussion and prayer together which remains relevant to the children as they grow up and develop in their own personal faith. This, while always difficult, is harder in modern society because of the different philosophies that children are exposed to, and the lengthening of the age of childhood, and the increased sophistication of our children in this generation.

3.  *School.* The family finds it difficult that the children face bullying at school because they are different. The different ethos of secular life, necessary though it might be, does cause difficulties for the children.

# Part Four
## WHAT NOW?

# 9

# *An Application of the Principles*

There is an enormous gap between the world of the Old Testament and that of twenty-first century Western civilisation. When so much of the Old Testament is culturally linked, it is hard to extend the principles into our very different culture. Nevertheless, this is the task of this chapter.

## 1. Making the application to today

It is possible to make the extension across the cultures in three areas of life. We have good biblical grounds for doing this.

### (a) The family

The family was, and remains, the basis of society in God's plan of the world. Any principles relating to the family are likely to be relevant throughout cultures and time, as God's plan for humanity is bigger than cultures and time. However, we run into certain difficulties as modern society is rapidly undoing the wider family (and even the nuclear one) and its responsibility for childcare. There may be problems in applying the principles through sheer lack of family members of the right spiritual calibre.

## (b) The parents

Secondly, it is also possible to talk of the role of parents, who have had a similar responsibility through the ages. Again some of the pressures that a modern child and parent face are vastly different, but the principles for dealing with them remain the same as in Old Testament times.

## (c) The support of God's people

Thirdly, it is also possible to extend these principles from the nation of Israel (God's people) to the church of today. The writer to the Hebrews (who was using powerfully Jewish images) describes the church in Hebrews 3:2–6 as God's house, just as Israel had been described for example in Numbers 12:7. This image of the nation, however, is perhaps a misleading one. The Old Testament idea of 'nation' is a bit different from our current nationalism. For Israel, 'nation' was simply the ultimate family group – family in the widest sense. Their expectation of relationships within the nation leant on the function of the Jewish household. Within the larger family there was security, religious nurture, teaching and worship. The action of one became the action of all, particularly if that one was the head. When he entered into an agreement or acted in some other way, the entire family was counted as having acted.[1]

So Jewish children looked to their parents first, then to the wider family, then to the clan, tribe, and nation. All these elements supplied support, leading and guidance under God.

---

1   *The Illustrated Bible Dictionary*, (IVP, 1980), p. 141.

This describes something of the function and system of the church as it should act today. The local church can become the extended family. Its life and fellowship enable individual family units to find support and encouragement within the collection of families gathered together as the local church.[2] The modern church environment should provide the role of family at the local level, and on a broader church base (perhaps at inter-church events) it should fulfil the role of clan and tribe, and then at national events it should fulfil the role of the nation.

*Summary*

So there are at least three very important areas where the principles of the Old Testament care for children are applicable to us in our society. These are nation, family and parents, and they relate to a modern pattern of the church family (both local and national), and the parents. With the changes in society over the last hundred years, the wider family of the Old Testament is not reproduced in modern Western society, but can be accepted under the role of local church.

## 2. Changes in society

'"The time is coming," declares the LORD, "when I will make a new covenant with the house of Israel"' (Jeremiah 31:31). There have also been changes in society which will affect the way we apply the principles and practices we have considered. The shift away from extended to nuclear families has meant that families have frequently lacked support and help which in previous generations would have been supplied by relatives and especially grandparents. This has become increasingly

---

2 *Ibid.*, p. 143.

true as families have become geographically more mobile.

The Old Testament ideal where there were grandparents and older people whose wisdom was much admired, as well as many uncles and aunts, mature cousins and so on, around, who could all add to the spiritual growth and encouragement of the child, is no longer usual in most of our societies.

So, for better or worse, the change in society means that the church has to accept a greater responsibility and role in replacing the wider family's influence. This is a huge burden, and it requires a large level of social interaction within the families of each church to build friendships and respect through which this sort of influence can be extended.

### (a) The church's role

If the church now has the same role to play as the extended family in the ancient world, then we also need to consider *how* the church can help in the education and training of our children. Much of this training has to be at home, but children should have the confidence of the wider family or church supporting them in the same teaching and behaviour. If this is to happen, the church needs to be aware of the presence of these children and find ways to cater for them, so they will feel they are part of it from their youngest days until they are virtually adults.[3]

(i) Children in church   This in itself calls for a careful attitude from the church congregation and its leaders. We must recognise that there are problems in having young children in a congregation at worship. Their behaviour is likely to be erratic: calling out during the quietness of a prayer time, crying, pulling the hymn books to pieces, and wandering

---

3   Eric Lane, *Special Children?*, p. 139.

around.[4] Yet we have also said that it is necessary for them to be there.

It is difficult for some to worship in such an environment, and it particularly disturbs the concentration of parents who seek to look after the children, as well as those unused to children, who may prefer quieter meditation in worship. The parents can be torn, knowing that disciplining their noisy youngster may bring more noise than the original misbehaviour; and the anger generated in the parents at their children's behaviour does not help their own worship (let alone the members of the congregation sitting nearby).

Because of this some parents are tempted to keep their children at home, or the church organises crèches or separate activities for the children. The motivation for this provision is the curing of a distraction, rather than for a better evangelistic or teaching environment.

Understandable and commendable though these efforts are, they are not the best answer to the problem of distracting children. This simply reinforces the idea that worship is for adults only. It also creates congregations without children. It gives the child a wrong message about church being a place where they are restricted and disciplined. It is better if parents can persevere and endure the hardship for a little while (see R. Buckland, *Children and God,* p.101). It is also better if the church can adapt and include the children, without excluding other groups. These two objectives might seem mutually exclusive, but some congregations have managed to cure the problems at least partially.

If the church is to be seen as the extended family of the ancient world, then it has to accept children for what they are, and give them the space and opportunities that a family

---

4  *Ibid.,* p. 142.

gathering would ordinarily allow. There is a need for seriousness and adult organisation, but within the family community
of the church the children have a valid and important contri-
bution, which must be recognised and allowed to be
expressed. Here we need to learn from the Old Testament
model and think of the things available in worship for the Old
Testament child. Children are able (if allowed) to bring their
own gifts to worship. We need to make our corporate worship
more real, more visual, more understandable, more sponta-
neous, more informal, more inclusive, more immediate and,
above all, more accessible to our children to participate in.

In worship children need:

- to be acknowledged as relevant, with a place together
  with their parents to worship;
- to hear preaching and prayers that relate to their lives,
  their hopes and their fears, as well as to those of the
  adults around them;
- to sing hymns without complex metaphors or tunes;
- to be allowed to have an attention span which moves in
  and out of focus quickly;
- to be directed into times of silence;
- to contribute appropriately from time to time;
- to see adults being both excited and honest about the
  Christian life.

Any attempts to integrate family worship, however, need to be
done carefully and prayerfully. Imagine for a moment the
scenario where a church decides that it will take action next
Sunday morning, and institute an all-age service. Apart from
the reaction of the older members of the congregation, whose
needs are already being met and who will now be more
marginalised, there are real problems for the children too. It

can be very difficult for children coming out of a Sunday school environment to come straight into an all-age event, especially in a large church. It is almost impossible to expect primary age children to feel part of this, unless they have their parents or their specialist group leader around them, participating with them. Now suddenly they find that belonging to the church is not simply belonging to Jesus but joining in an activity where they do not understand everything.[5]

Simply importing a different worship style is not an instant fix.

*(ii)  Special interest groups*    Obviously children are only one special interest group within the church, and should not be pampered in a way that destroys another group's participation.

A wise church will seek to meet the needs of *all* its interest groups, and promote harmony, love and understanding within each of the groups. No one group's needs should be allowed to dominate the agenda of the church, whether that be the young, the youth, the young married couples, the elderly, the new converts, the unsaved, or any of the multiple possibilities of interest groups.

Yet within the space of the church's week, there should be special slots catering for the needs of all these groups specifically, and then some time when all of them can come together and worship God, showing the unity and strength which comes from such diverse experience. Here the needs of each group will have to be met at least on a rota basis, if not all within the one meeting. Such statements might appear radical, but they only show how far we are from taking the needs of our special interest groups seriously. Israel saw the

---

5   Penny Frank, *Children and Evangelism*, p. 55.

need for children to be involved in worship, and gave the space for that to happen regularly within the worship of the people.

## (b) The parent

Other changes in society affect the role of the parent. In the ancient world, the child remained with the parent to learn life skills. Nowadays the child goes to school to learn those skills instead. This is because modern society is considerably more complex and children require greater input and training in order to survive in the modern world and choose from all the options now available to them. We saw in the chapter on child psychology that there are many influences and pressures brought to bear on our children these days and few of them are Christian ones.

Old Testament children had the double barrier of nation and family to protect them from the wider world and its pressures. Our children have only the church, and their immediate family. While these are adequate for a while, once state education begins the child is suddenly exposed to a whole range of other opinions and behaviour patterns. These have a greater impact on the child who considers church (if they go at all) to be an irritating irrelevance, or at best a place where they go and play with their friends. A child who has already discovered that God is a real and loving person who is there for him, and who accepts his praise and prayers, will have some measure of insulation from this. Even so, it is tough for these children; and even tougher for those without that support.

Above all that, there is a new attitude to the older generations these days: they are useless, behind the times, and cannot have any ideas about life. Perhaps such a view stems from the technological age we live in, where it is difficult to keep in touch with modern advances, and the older generations find it particularly so. Whatever the case, it means that people beyond our own generation are not considered to be worth seeking advice from. The parents are 'past it' and don't understand the needs of the child, and probably also don't really understand some of the things that the child is being taught in school. There is therefore no encouragement for the child to seek help from either their parents or the church, because they are seen as simply not relevant. All this compounds the problems of parenting today.

We have seen that the role of the church is important here to train and protect the children, making them feel at home, relevant, and part of the church. However, they do not carry the main responsibility. The church has not replaced the parent as the main teacher of the children; it has replaced the extended family, and the nation. Therefore the role of the parent is still primary and the responsibilities that the parents in the Old Testament had still apply today. We are still required to educate them in the ways of the Lord.

The term used in the Old Testament means 'train; nurture' and is applicable to plants and animals as well as children. All need much care and attention lavished upon them if they are to grow properly. This is entrusted to parents according to Scripture and should not be delegated to schools or other such institutions.[6] So while the job of parenting may have got harder, it does not excuse the parents, and allow them to ditch the responsibility onto the church or state.

We as parents, church leaders and children's workers should still be teaching them what the Scriptures say. The parents should do this because they still have the best opportunity. The children remain with them day after day for many years and can learn from the parents' attitudes and

---

6   Eric Lane, *Special Children?*, pp. 113–114.

approaches to things. In our society, as has been noted already, the child quickly becomes exposed to the range of human experience from schoolfriends, and playmates. The demands of education and play all take the children much further away from the parent emotionally, intellectually and physically than ever before. All this means that the parent has less contact with the child, and that the child receives input from wider sources, whose presentation of spiritual matters may well be unacceptable to us. This all makes the role of the parent more crucial in the smaller amounts of time that they have with their children. Christian parents will want their children not only to keep on the rails morally but also to come to faith in Christ. They need to be careful about all they say and do which has any bearing, directly or indirectly, upon their children.[7] The children *must* be able to see God in the home because they will be unlikely to see him in the play-ground. Of course, there are good organisations working to reach the child even there, but once again these are ancillary organisations. The main responsibility remains with the parent.

Here again the church has a role to play. The pastor and the elders do all they can to help the parents fulfil their oblig-ation to bring up their children in the training and instruction of the Lord. The best way is for the pastor to teach the parents 'all the counsel of God'.[8]

*Summary*

The church and parents today have to take their responsi-bility more seriously, accepting their role as models for the children to copy. They have a responsibility to act more in line

---

7  *Ibid.*, p. 110.
8  *Ibid.*, p. 137.

with the care and priorities that the Old Testament people gave to their children. How is this to be achieved? We need to think once again about stages of child development.

## 3. An application to our practice of childcare

'Your ears will hear a voice behind you, saying, "This is the way; walk in it"' (Isaiah 30:21). Taking the three stages of child development we used as standard in Chapter 6, we can now apply the lessons learned from the Jewish system to our modern church systems of reaching children.

*(a) Emotional: stage 1* (up to around six years old, the pre-school and early school years)

Here the Jews simply involved the children in every detail of Jewish worship, both at home and in the public gatherings. There were no 'special' children's meetings, and the children were not drawn into separate areas to allow peace in the public meetings (though if children were overly disruptive the women took them out). We have already noticed, however, that the public worship of God was much more visual and symbol-centred than it is in modern churches. It was a lot easier for children to participate in worship services. They were encouraged to ask the meanings of the symbols, and then join in themselves in whatever way the specific festival required.

This was true of home worship as well. The family would gather together and talk of God in their day-to-day activities. Again, family worship was based on visual images and was heavy with symbolism, and the children were encouraged to take part with questions and actions.

The church approach to this today is very different. Generally under-sixes are considered to need only a baby-

sitting service. This is because they are too young to understand the gospel and therefore are not really part of the
church at all. Modern theory certainly accepts that they can
demonstrate faith, and indeed we all accept that they do so in
all kinds of different things. The church needs to learn to
accept this, and encourage it among the very young. All six-
year-olds (no matter how good or bad their parents are) are
able to demonstrate a faith in their parents. 'Daddy mend it'
is a common cry, no matter how battered the favourite toy is;
the child has absolute confidence that Daddy can mend
*anything*. If the child can have that sort of faith in his parents,
then we should be able to accept that a faith in God is
possible as well. There is sometimes little effort to try and
teach faith or discipleship at this age; the church does not
usually consider these lessons of modern psychological theories of education, or Jewish practices.

Furthermore, parents with little time at their disposal do
not usually involve the children in all that they are doing, nor
do they bring God into their daily existence. Substitutes such
as a secular nursery, school, TV and video, and the home
computer have replaced this for some parents. While there is
nothing wrong with any of these things in and of themselves,
this does represent a major shift away from the pattern of
Jewish society, where the parents moulded the attitudes of the
child by being present, involving the child in their activities,
and teaching them about the world as they see it, not as
Nintendo or Disney sees it.

*(b) Intellectual: stage 2* (5–11-year-olds, the infant and junior
school age)

The Jews were starting to introduce their children to the
Scriptures at this point, telling the children more about God,
from God's own word now, rather than from the daily life

experiences of the home. They would still be involved in the public worship of the nation, which was still very visual, and participation-centred. At home this would continue, with the child being encouraged to memorise Scriptures and learn the history of the people. That would not be a dry dusty date after date type of history, but real stories of the past where God did something exciting for the children's parents and grandparents, in places near where they lived. It would be a practical and relevant history.

The church today does relate better to this age group, but tends to do so by isolating them in their own special meeting. In the public worship times, this age group tends to be addressed for a short period of time by the speaker. This is a short message often with a visual aid, and often about a biblical theme or doctrine. 'Object lesson' talks are the usual books written for ministers to help with this, and attempt to teach things like the Trinity by using ice, water and steam, for example. The subject matter tends to be ideas rather than concrete stories and histories with practical application. This is very different from both the Jewish and modern psychological approach, which suggest that children of this age are usually incapable of understanding these things in a meaningful way. The church is attempting to communicate with the child, but often fails to teach truths about God that the child can comprehend, and in a way the child can understand. Children need more practical subjects and stories with a relevant application for them.

The children then go out to Sunday school, which is usually better aimed at their abilities, and Bible stories are taught. The relationship of the Sunday school teachers with the children here is crucial, as they become role models for the children. It is well known that most adults can remember their Sunday school teacher, but few can remember what they taught. So the life of those teachers, and the relevance of what they are teaching to everyday life, is crucial to the way that the child will learn from them. The Jews appointed their best teachers to the children. The rabbis had some twenty-four years of learning, and then went and taught in the schools. The Jews believed that they were investing in the future, securing another generation's obedience to the covenant faith of God. The church often does not. Sunday school teaching is often given to the young female teenagers in the church merely to give them something to do in an effort to keep them in the church, and to make them feel useful. There is rarely any training given to these people. In fact, until recently, there have been very few organisations willing to offer training for them.

Outside the main worship services, there is sometimes also a midweek event, which is usually better attended and staffed than the Sunday schools. This time the people doing it are usually the enthusiasts, the ones who have a vision for children and really care enough to give up a weekday evening. Here again, the teachers tend to be role models, and children learn more from them than they do from the teaching. It is perhaps no surprise then that these meetings are generally more successful in attracting, holding, and teaching children, especially those from unchurched backgrounds, than the other services are. Modern society and its attitude to Sundays and family days may also play a part in being able to attract numbers to these clubs, but not to Sunday schools. Nevertheless, the teaching and relevance of the club has to hold the children and speak to them. This group is probably the closest the church comes to matching modern methods. It also matches the Old Testament pattern of the wider family where children of similar age would play together and be encouraged in Jewish things by their older friends and neighbours.

Once again in the home, things are not usually very close to the Jewish or psychological patterns of education. The stories from the Bible may be read alongside Peter Rabbit or the Famous Five and the child cannot separate fact from fiction. There may be little reality of God visible in the life of the family supporting the teaching that the parents do try to give in the home. So while Christian parents do teach about God, the end result is often confusion rather than certainty. There is nothing wrong with Peter Rabbit, but the child must be able to see from the parents' lives that Jesus matters to them, and is involved in their lives, while Peter Rabbit is not. What the parents think about Jesus must be visible in what they say and do all the time, not just in front of the children.

Added to that, the child is picking up all sorts of things from school and TV, usually without the balance of strong Christian standards in the home. This can lead to rebellion and a rejection of the parents' standards, which ultimately means a rejection of God. Alternatively, at this age, the parents can become severe, dictating what the children can watch, where they can go, with whom they can be seen, and imposing standards that they have not known before, and do not see their peer group living by. They see no reason to obey – at least not one they can understand as valid ('because I say so' is never an acceptable reason to a child). The rules are based on principles that they cannot understand, and have not had taught to them in a loving way from the stories and worship of the church from infancy. In short the restrictions seem unfair to the child, and the seeds of rebellion begin here too.

An approach taken by some is to remove the child from outside influences altogether by home education and isolation. The child may learn their social skills in the church environment (providing there are enough other youngsters their own age, and that they relate to them often enough). However, this is also fraught with danger, as the child then grows up unaware of the issues in the world, and unable to cope with them when he goes out into the world, and as a young adult suddenly becomes aware of things he had no idea about before. Survival at this stage is very difficult unless they have some foundations of experience on which to lean. They are like a plant grown in a greenhouse suddenly exposed to a winter storm. They have grown well and beautifully in the lovely conditions, but as soon as they are exposed to the world's conditions, they cannot survive because they are not acclimatised to them. We are training our children to be Christians in the real world. The best training we can give them is to show them how we can cope being Christians 'out there'. We have to show them how Jesus helps us, and how and when we need to follow Jesus instead of the world's ways of doing things. (This is not meant as a critique of the Christian school system, but it does highlight some dangers of it, which I know some of the Christian schools are aware of.) This means that children have to be exposed to the world carefully and gradually, protected by a buffer of knowing that Mum and Dad have 'been there, done that' and that Jesus has helped them get through it.

*(c) Volitional: stage 3* (eleven plus, secondary school age group)

At this stage, the Jews started to teach the children the Commandments and more abstract ideas. They were given more responsibility. Many of them would soon be working full-time, and all were helping full-time in the family home. The emphasis on public worship remained the same, and at this age the children would start to understand the reasons for the symbols that they had been seeing all these years.

They had always been told the reasons, but now the system was coming together into a logical reality for them. It all started to make sense, and hopefully they would be continuing in this faith which they had always followed, out of a logical choice, a personal identification with it, which would find expression in the Bar Mitzvah.

The church generally does better at this stage, because it can often understand the needs of this age group better than it can those of the younger ones. This age group can understand and use logic, and many adults feel more comfortable talking on this level. The child is finally equipped to cope with the concepts used in their spiritual talks (though the teenager may well feel patronised by them now). The main services of the church are now more understandable for the child. However, they may still be out in Sunday school doing things that are getting to be too simple for them and becoming bored. If they are in Sunday school, it needs to become a discussion group preparing them for looking carefully at passages and learning from them. It should be a stepping stone into the main Sunday services.

If they are in the main service already, the probability is that they will not be catered for at all in the service, and will therefore not be quite capable of understanding all that is happening. The service will be based around a lengthy talk, difficult to follow unless you are motivated to do so, and also music which the young people will probably consider irrelevant, if not arcane. The teenagers will need to learn how to learn at this level. They are doing that at school, and will need to make the same transition in the church. It is not easy, and takes time. The church needs to consider ways of helping them do this.

The church, in order to help, does often allocate resources to this area by providing youth workers, resources, and appropriate training. This means that the calibre of work among this age group is generally good. On the other hand, the children already have preconceptions of 'church' and 'God' which might not be very helpful, due to their experience in earlier years.

In the special services the church also does quite well with this age group, both in helping them, and in reaching out to others. Sometimes, however, it is too little, too late. The children have not been taught from the beginning that God is real and important. Then, when faced with the ever-growing challenges of this age, the child can and does easily drift off to join a different peer group when the mood takes them. They will also have already rejected the advice of parents and the older members of the church as irrelevant, out of touch, and not helpful, possibly unnecessarily restrictive. Christianity does not relate well to the culture of the modern teenager, and modern children lack the good role models to copy that the Jewish system gave its young people.

Parents can also have their biggest problems with their children at this stage, if a relationship of talking, trust and including God consistently in everything has not been forged from the beginning. Even then, that is no automatic safeguard for the teenager, who may well decide to stop talking and accepting parental advice, simply because his peer group determines that it isn't 'cool', 'safe' or 'fat' (or whatever the current term might happen to be in any given week!). In fact, rebellion at this stage is the norm rather than the exception, which perhaps indicates what a poor job both parents and the church are doing generally. Our youth leaders are struggling to try and compensate for these problems, and there is an ever-growing focus on them as more and more churches are targeting this age group. I believe that this is really damage limitation. The damage is already done, and the church is fighting a battle against the odds. If the effort was put into parenting courses, and to children at an earlier stage, the results would more likely be significant. The old proverb 'A stitch in time saves nine' seems to be really appropriate here.

## Conclusion

In conclusion, then, the modern parent and the modern church are both failing to approach the evangelising of children in a way that makes sense, either from the Old Testament pattern held out for them, or from the educational psychologists of today. There is much that we, as churches and also as parents, need to think through in the way we try to teach and train our children.

# Bibliography

Berkhof, L., *Systematic Theology,* Banner of Truth 1939 (using the 1984 edition).

Bridger, F., *Children Finding Faith,* Scripture Union 1988.

Bruce, F. F., *The Spreading Flame,* Paternoster Press 1958.

Buckland, R., *Children of the King,* Anzea 1979.

Buckland, R., *Children and God,* Scripture Union 1938.

Butler, P., *Reaching Children,* Scripture Union 1992.

Clements, R.E., 'The relation of Children to the People of God in the Old Testament' in *Baptist Quarterly,* 21:5 (January 1966), pp.195–205.

Dallow, G., 'Children BC' in part 1 *Children's Ministry* magazine, Issue 5 1999.

Dallow, G., 'Children BC' in part 2 *Children's Ministry* magazine, Issue 6 1999.

Dallow, G., 'Children BC' in part 3 *Children's Ministry* magazine, Issue 7 1999.

Drane, J., *Introducing the Old Testament,* Lion 1987.

Dunn, J., *Romans 1–8 Word Biblical Commentary Series,* Vol. 38, Word 1988.

Dyter, R., *School Assemblies Need You!,* Monarch 1997.

Erickson, M. J., *Christian Theology,* Baker 1987.

Frank, P., *Children and Evangelism,* Marshall Pickering 1992.

Green, M., *Baptism, Its Purpose, Practice and Power,* Hodder & Stoughton 1987.

Grudem, W., *Systematic Theology: An Introduction to Biblical Doctrine,* IVP 1994.

Hendrickson, W., *The Bible in the Life Hereafter,* Baker 1959.

*Holman Bible Dictionary* in Quick Verse 4.0.

Honeycott, J., 'The Child within the Old Testament Community', in *Children and Conversion*, Broadman 1970.

*The Illustrated Bible Dictionary*, IVP 1980.

Inchley, J., *The Realities of Childhood*, Scripture Union 1985.

Lane, E., *Special Children? A Theology of Childhood,* Grace Publications 1996.

*The Lion Encyclopaedia of the Bible,* Lion 1978.

*The New Bible Dictionary,* Vol.1, IVP 1962.

Prince, J., *Whose Is the Kingdom?,* Scripture Union 1979.

Quick Verse 4.0 New Reference Bible Collection, Parsons Technology 1997.

Sanders, E. P., *Judaism Practice and Belief,* SCM Press 1992.

Schultz, Thom and Joani, *The Dirt on Learning*, Group Publishing 1995. (The information here was adapted from an older study completed by the Search Institute of America in the early 1990s. It was called Effective Christian Education. The study involved six US mainline Protestant denominations.)

Schultz, Thom and Joani, 'Seven Days a Week Teaching', in *Children's Ministry* magazine, Issue 7 1999.

Smale, I., *A History of Children,* Vol. 1, Silver Fish 1998.

Sprange, H., *Kingdom Kids,* Christian Focus 1994.

Stern, E., *Greek and Latin Authors on Jews and Judaism,* Vol. I. pp. 2–4, The Israel Academy of Sciences and Humanities 1984.

Strange, W. A., *Children in the Early Church,* Paternoster Press 1996.

Thompson, J. A., *Handbook of Life in Bible Times*, IVP 1986.

Westerhoff, J., *Will Our Children Have Faith?,* Seabury Press 1976.

Wood, A., *Judaism,* Batsford Academic and Educational Press 1984.

# Every Child: A Chance to Choose

## by Penny Frank

This book is about giving *all* children the opportunity to discover Jesus and to respond to him.

- What do children need to come to faith?
- How can we provide ongoing training for ministers and leaders?
- How can co-operation across the denominations become a reality?

Penny Frank looks at these and other critical issues for children's ministry today. Combining a positive assessment of church resources with a determined effort to trust the eternal promises of God, she holds out the prospect of a ministry that could transform our nation.

*'I commend this book by Penny Frank . . . because I believe these pages might help us all to dig beneath our actions and feelings to ask why we are still excluding so many children from the body of Christ.'*

James Jones
Bishop of Liverpool

**CHILDREN'S MINISTRY**

## CHILDREN'S MINISTRY

**Resources**

**ENHANCING YOUR MINISTRY WITH CHILDREN**

# Guides

GUIDE TO

## Using Dance and Drama

RUTH ALLISTON
Series Editor: SUE PRICE

GUIDE TO

## Dealing with Disruptive Children

ANDY BACK
Series Editor: SUE PRICE

GUIDE TO

## Tailored Teaching for 5-9s

SUE PRICE

GUIDE TO

## Storytelling

RUTH ALLISTON
Series Editor: SUE PRICE

# HELPING YOU REACH A NEW GENERATION

# *Children's Ministry Teaching Programme*

- Do you want to see children develop a personal relationship with Jesus?

- Do you want teaching sessions that are fun, biblical, evangelical and interactive?

- Would you like children to enjoy age-appropriate activities as they learn about God?

If you've said YES to any of these questions, you need the Children's Ministry Teaching Programme.

The Children's Ministry Teaching Programme provides four leader's guides covering ages from under 3 to 13+; KidZone activity books for children aged 5-7, 7-9 and 9-11; MiniKidz and KidZone craft books for children aged 3-5 and 5-9, a magazine for those over 11; a CD of music and stories; and FamilyZone with song words, ideas for all-age worship and parents' letters.

**For more information visit our web site
www.childrensministry.co.uk**